Le F #* % Vous JeSuis Occupé

Détente Coloriage Livre Edition

Coloring Bandit

Publié par Speedy Publishing Canada Limited

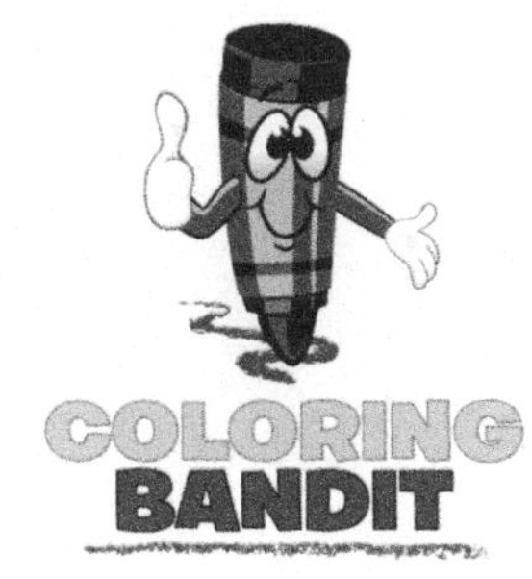

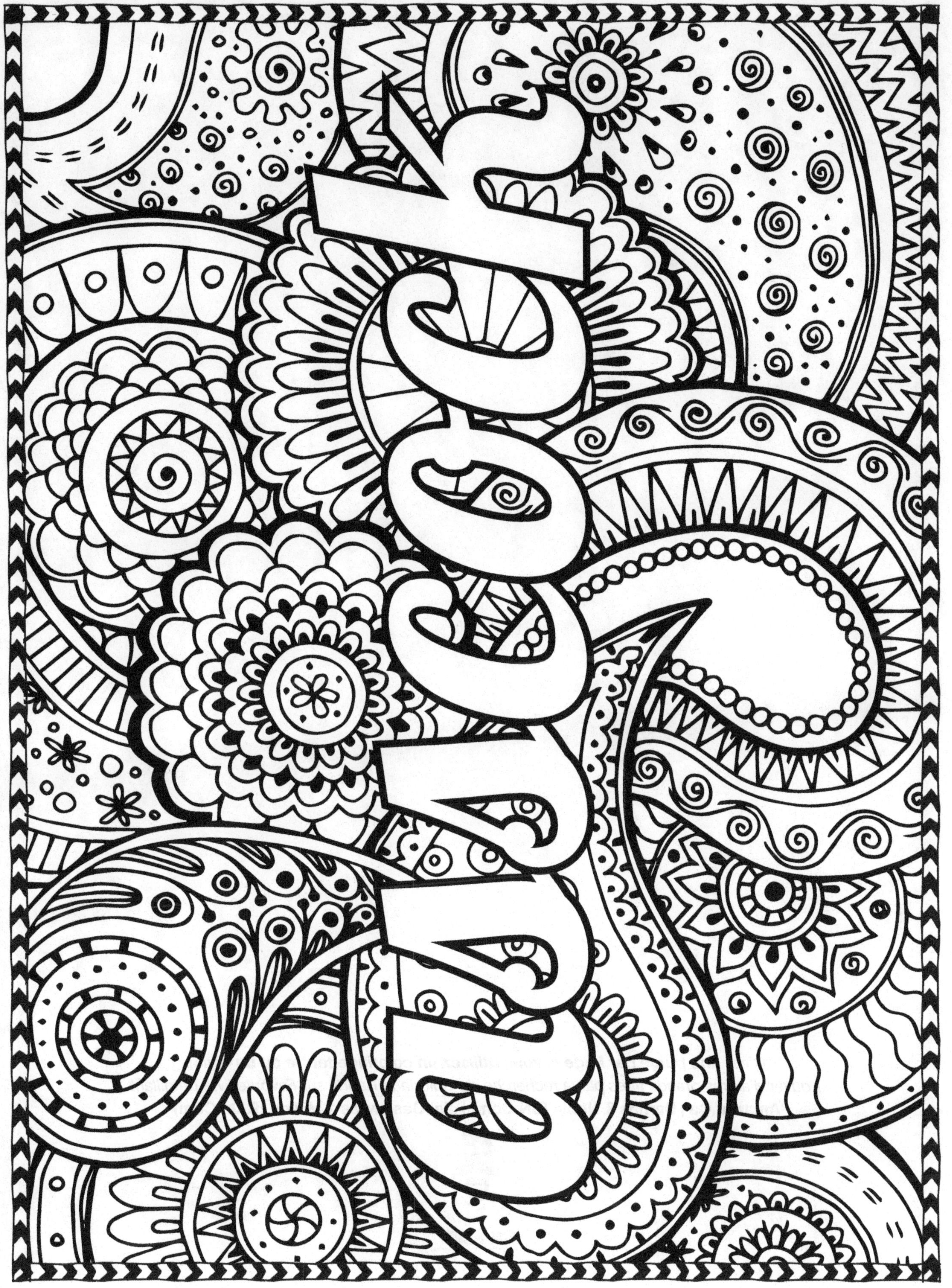

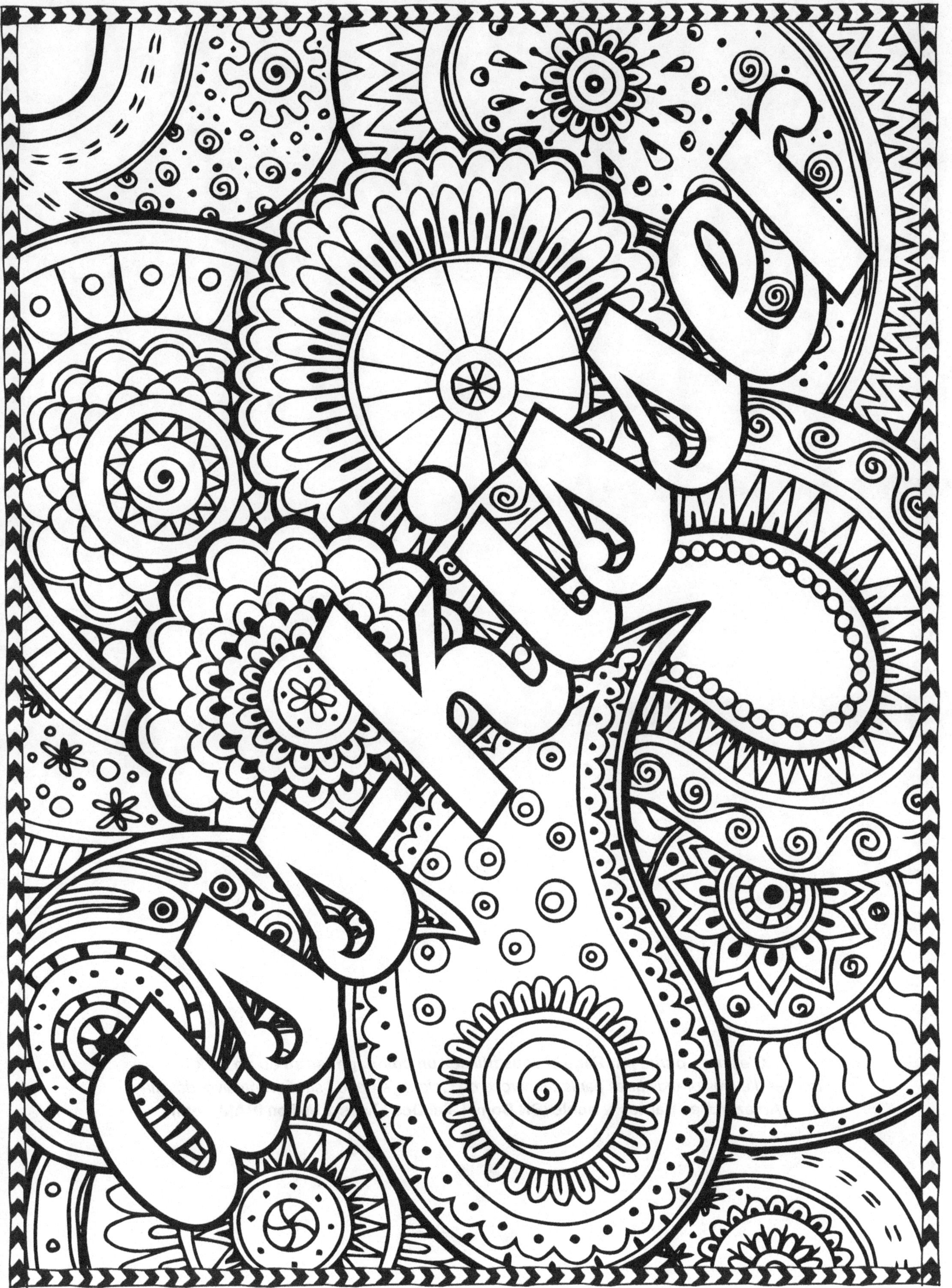

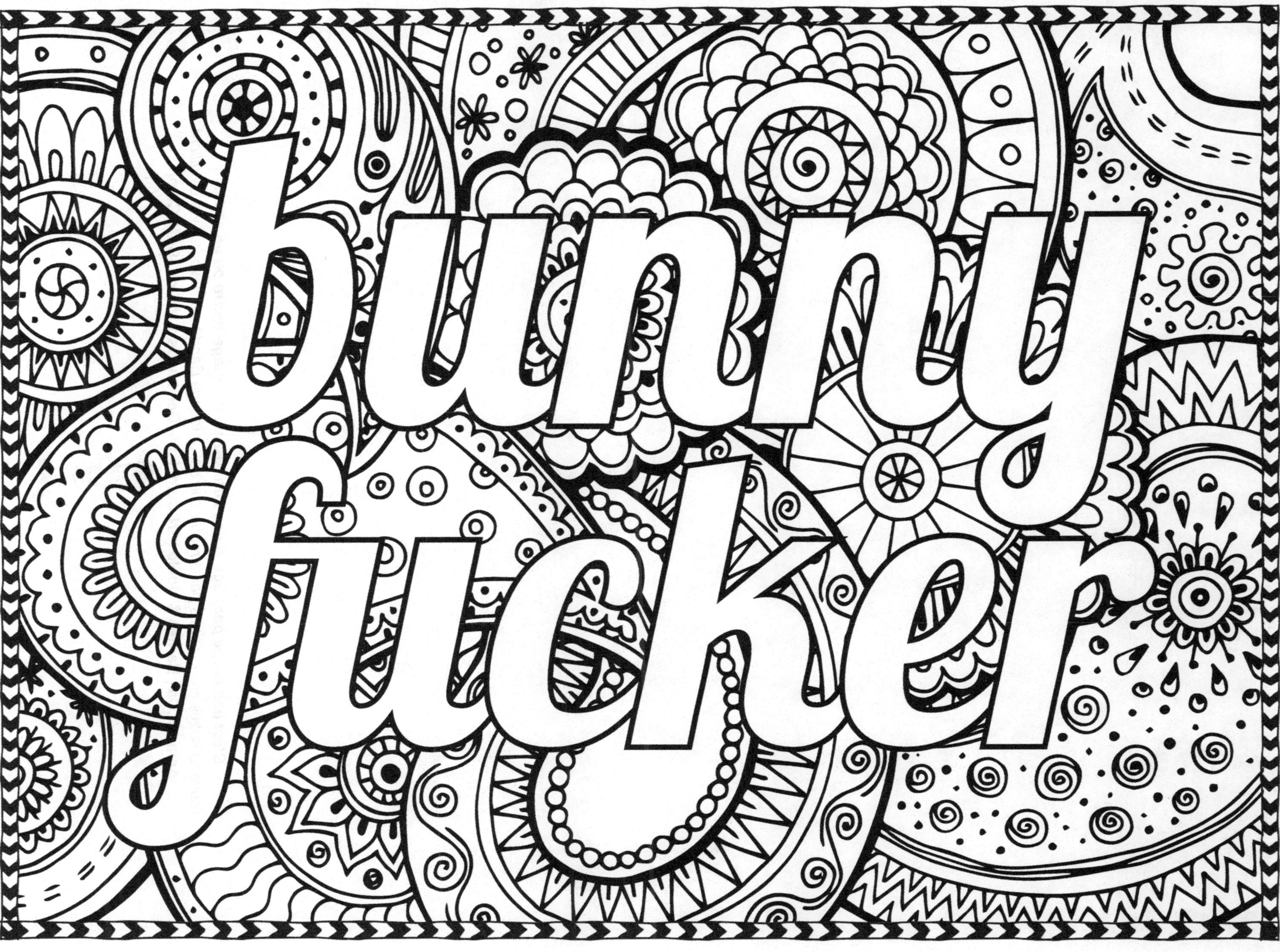

bunny fucker

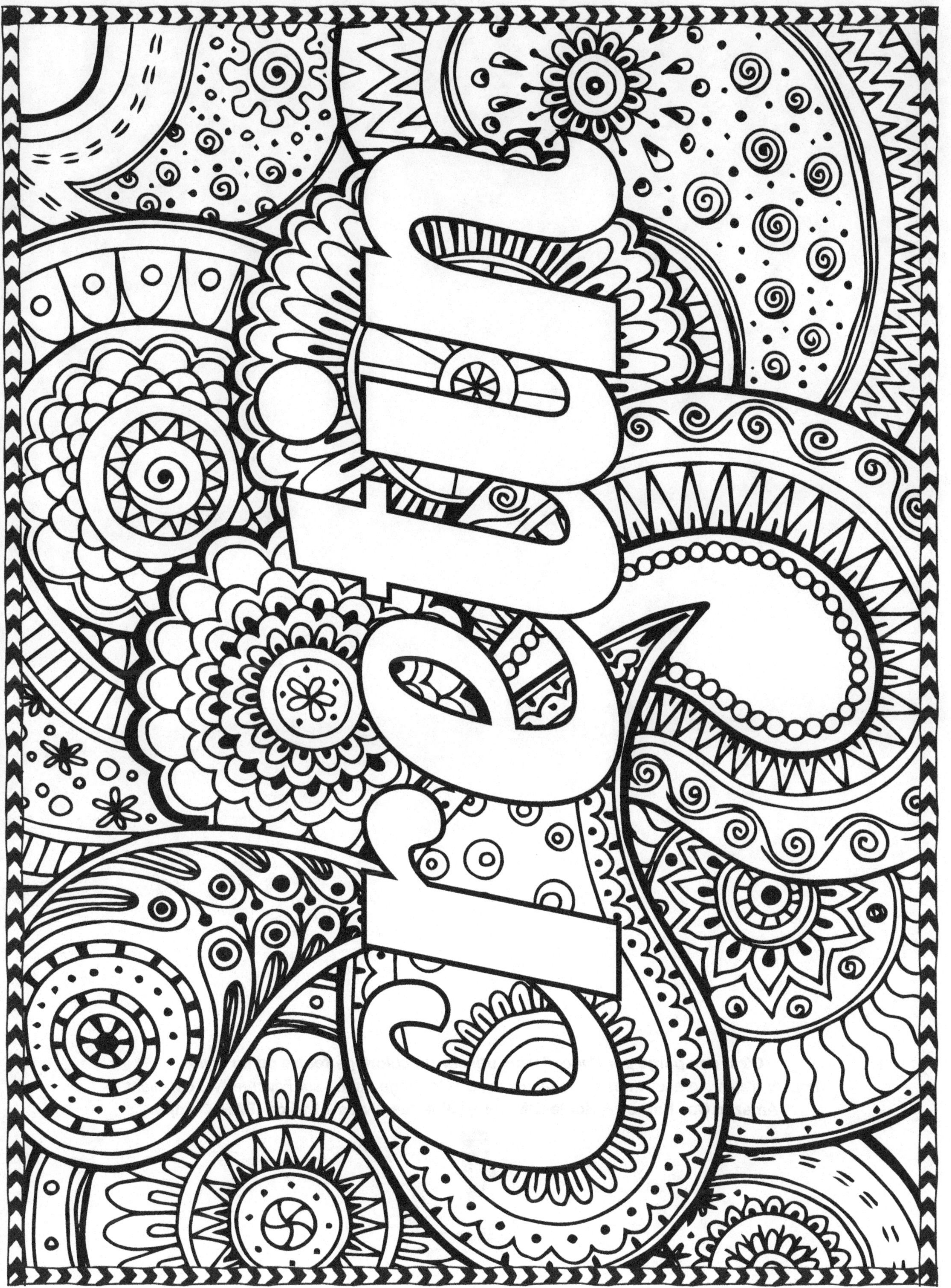
BITCH

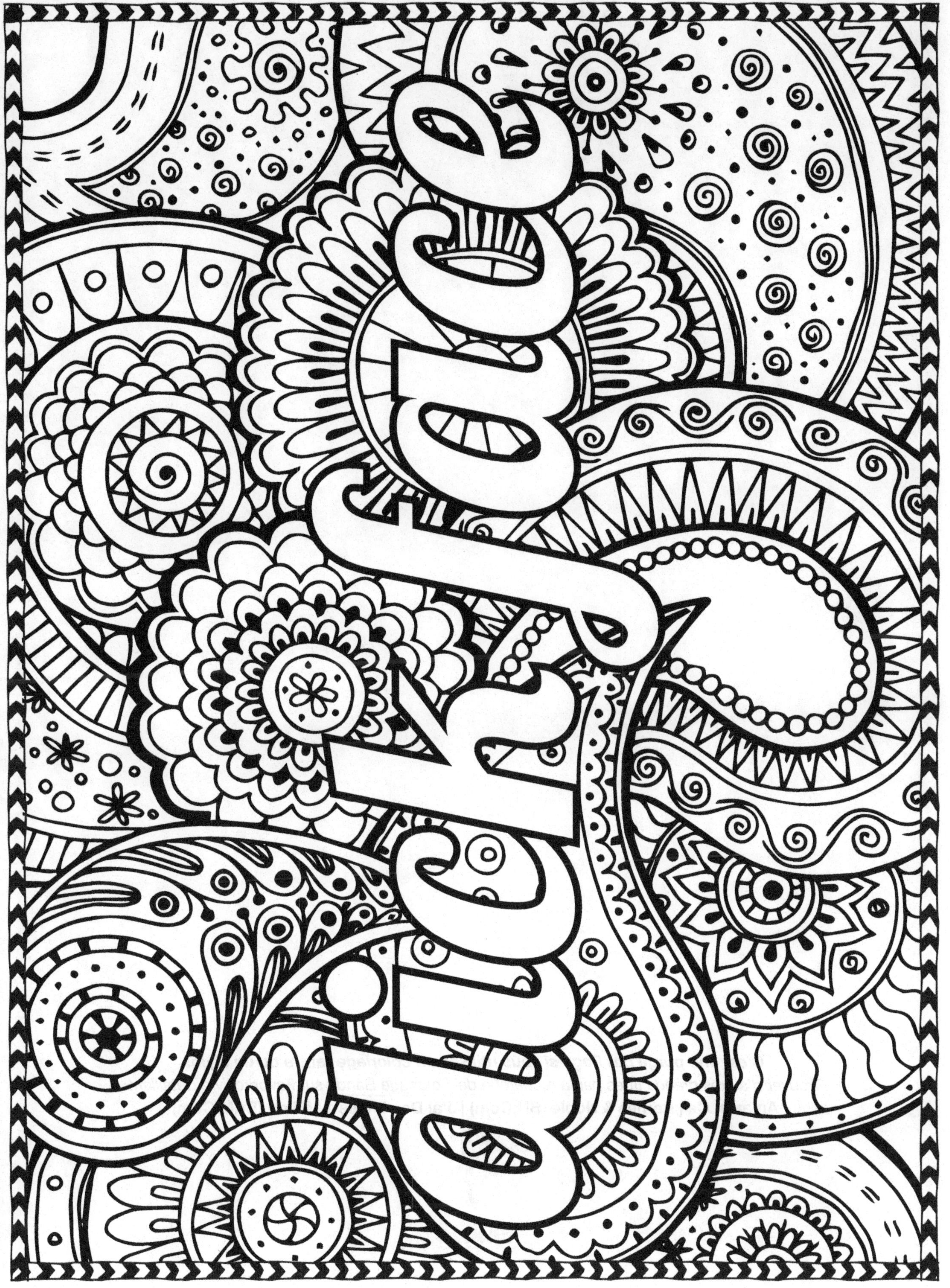

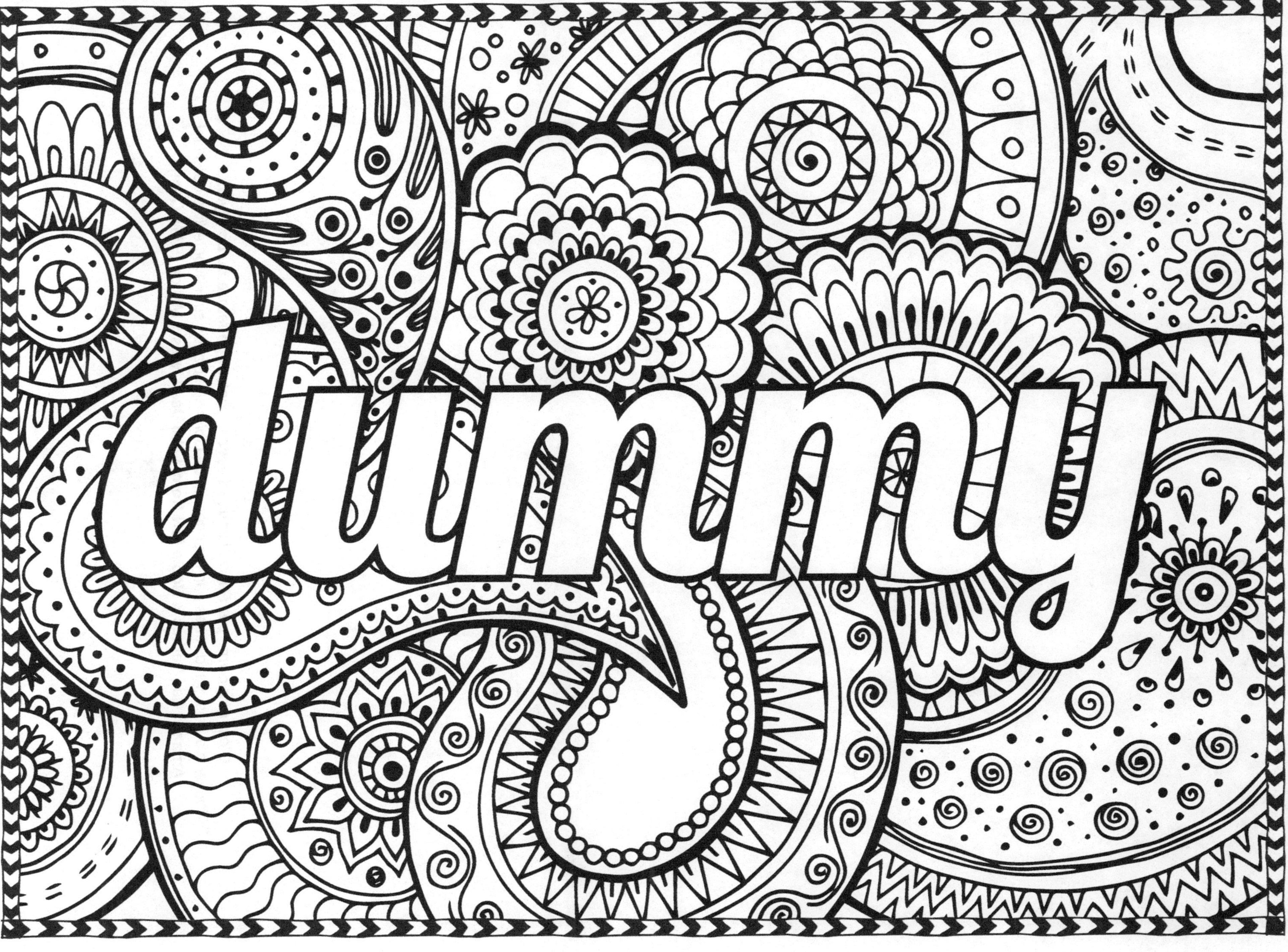

dummy

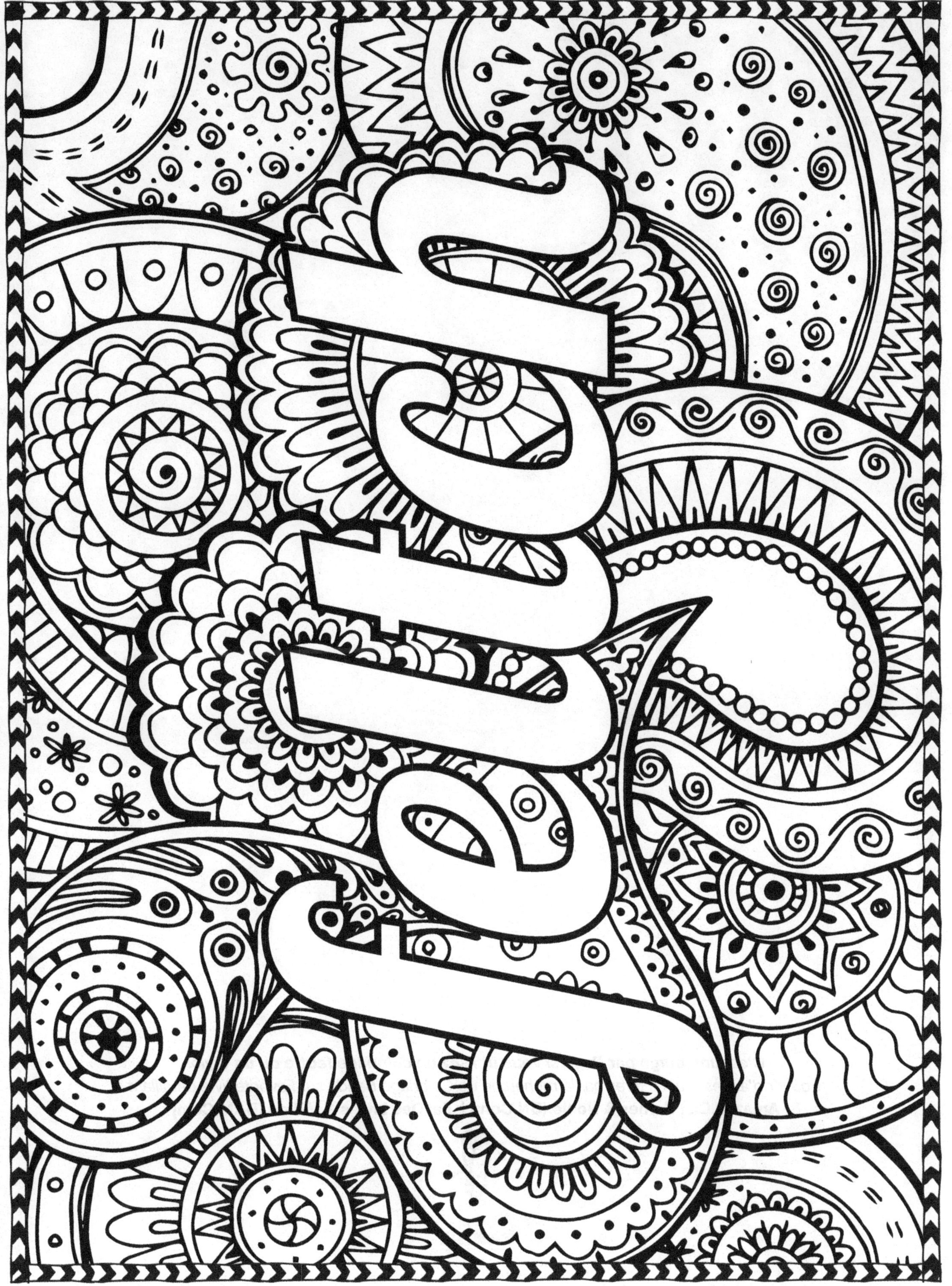

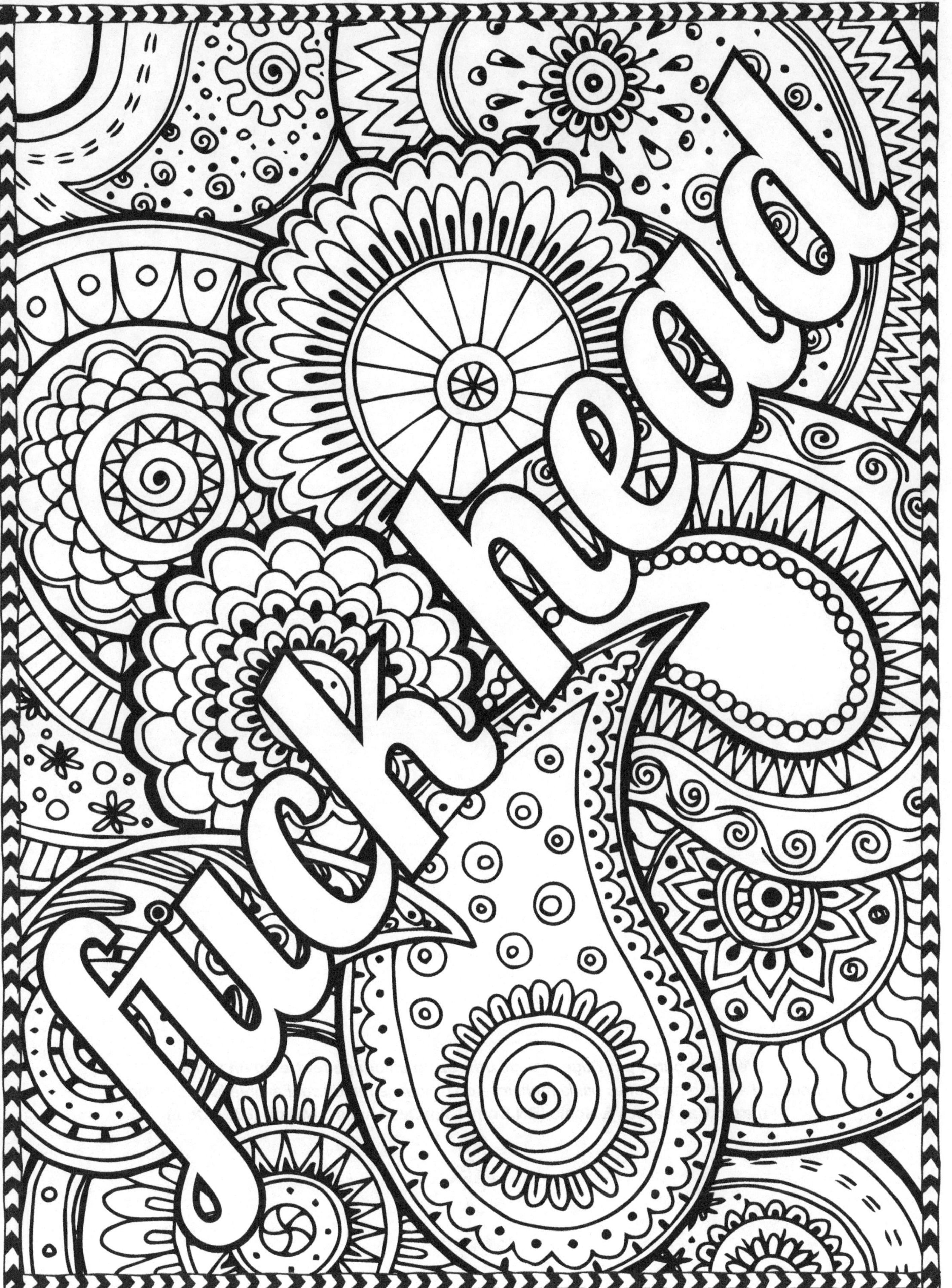

fuck head

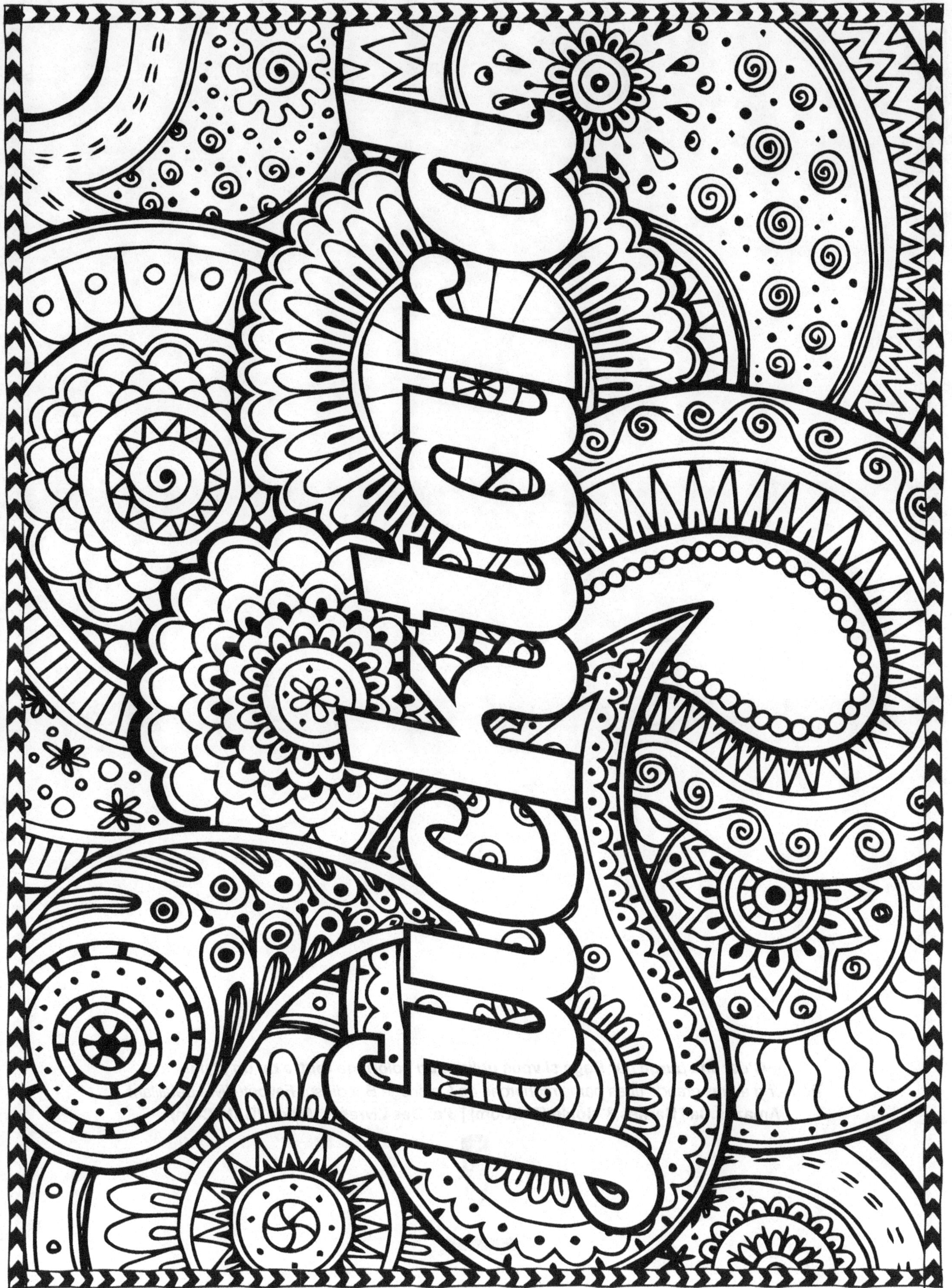

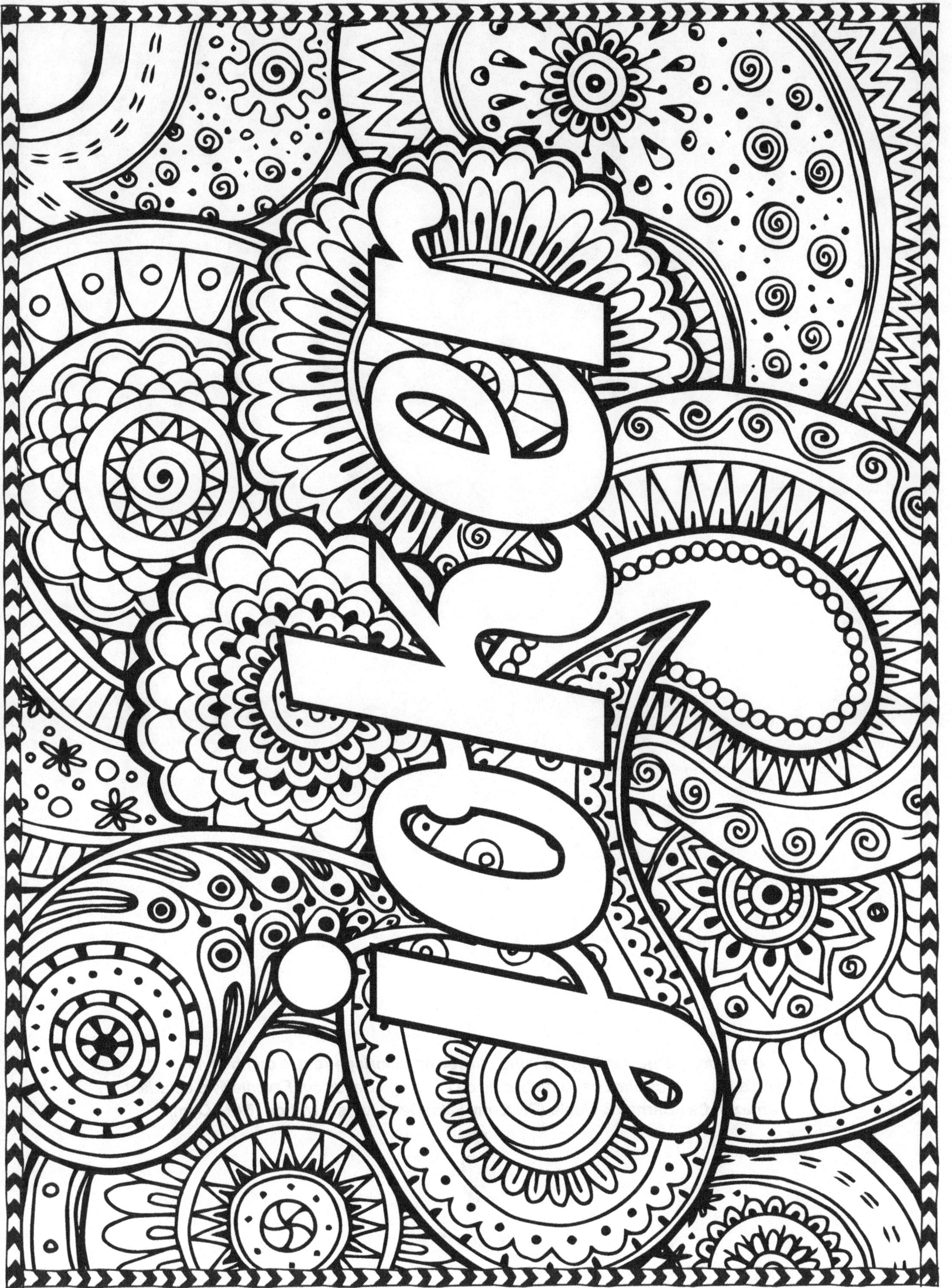

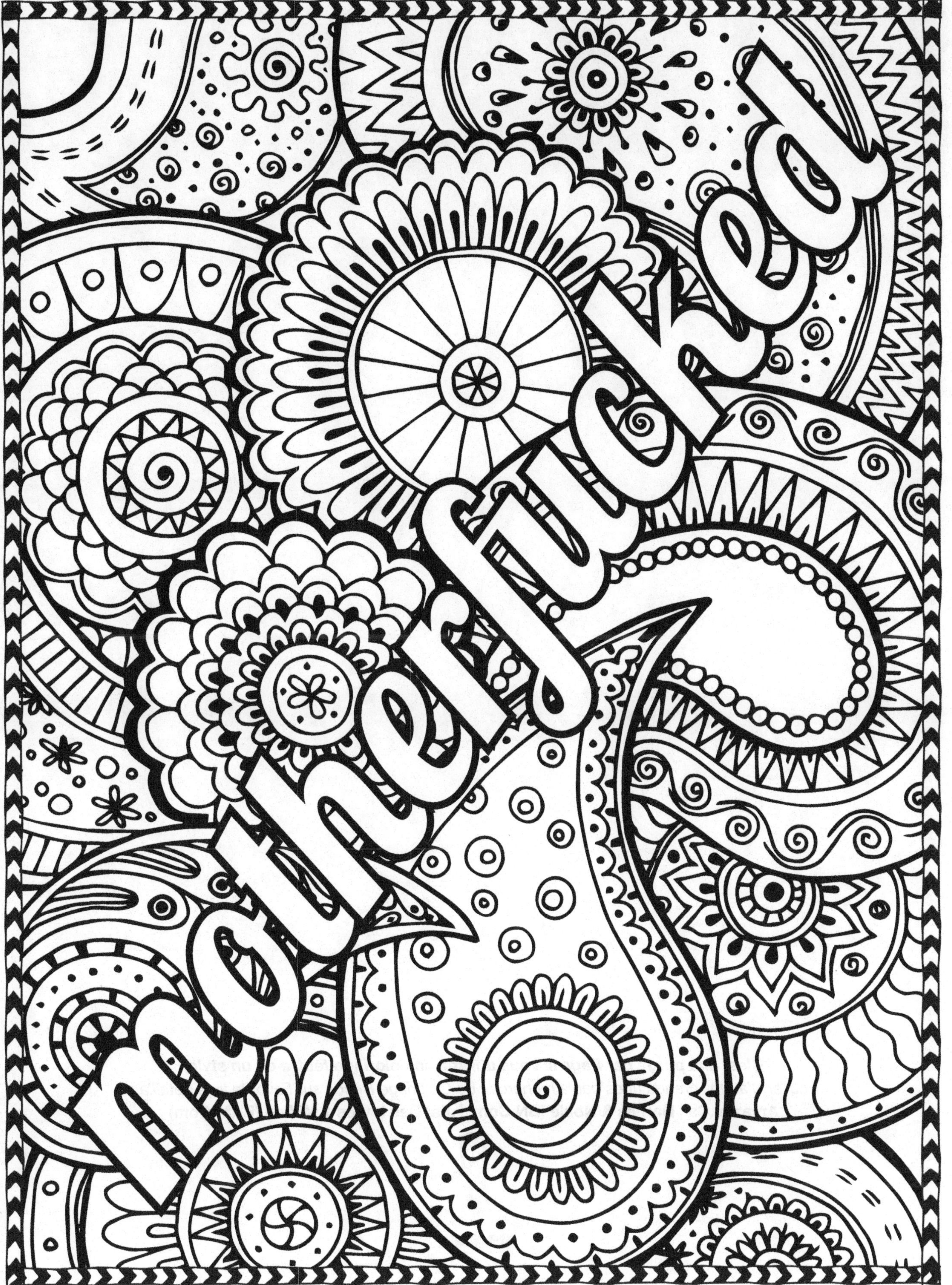
motherfucked

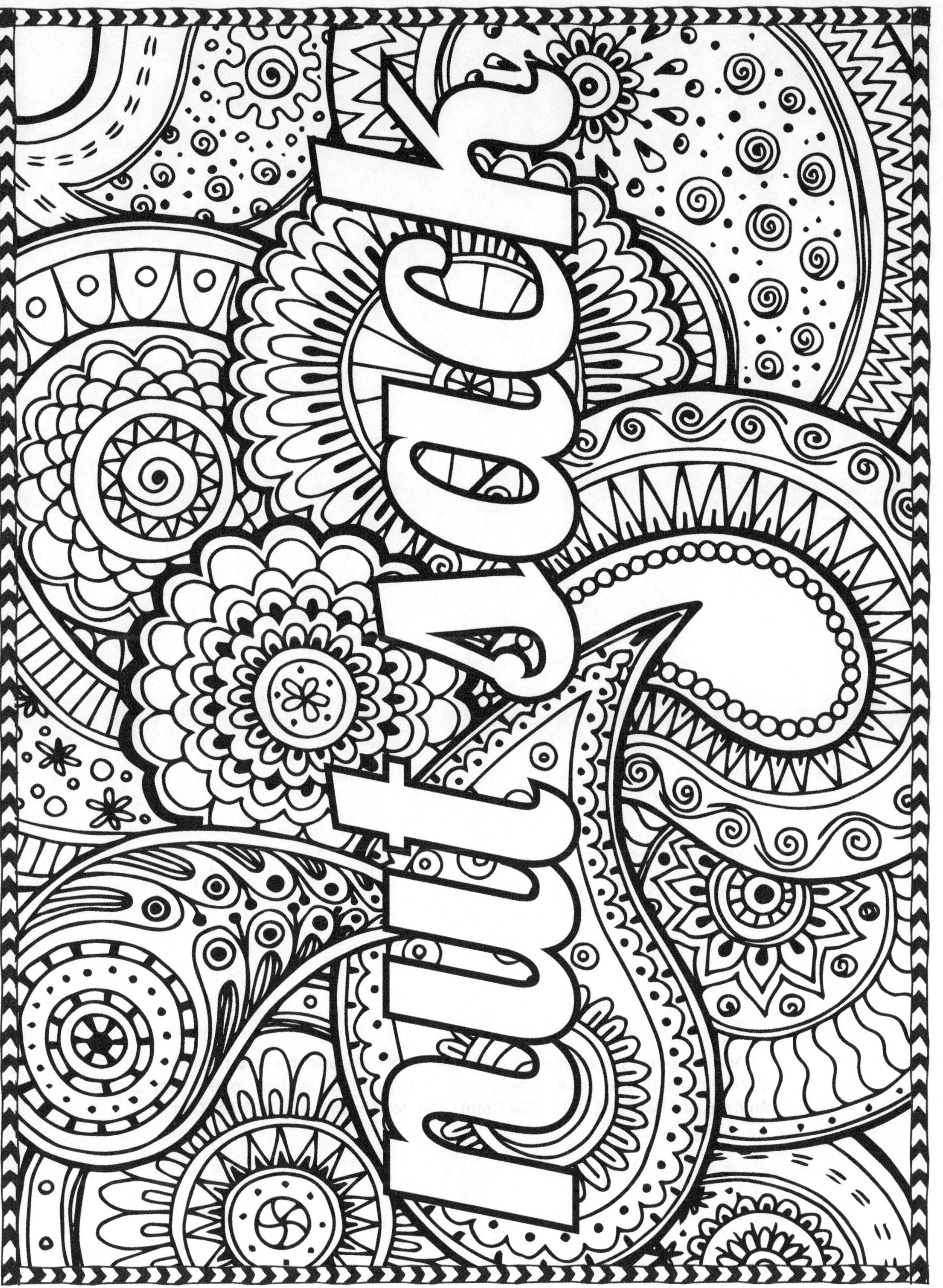

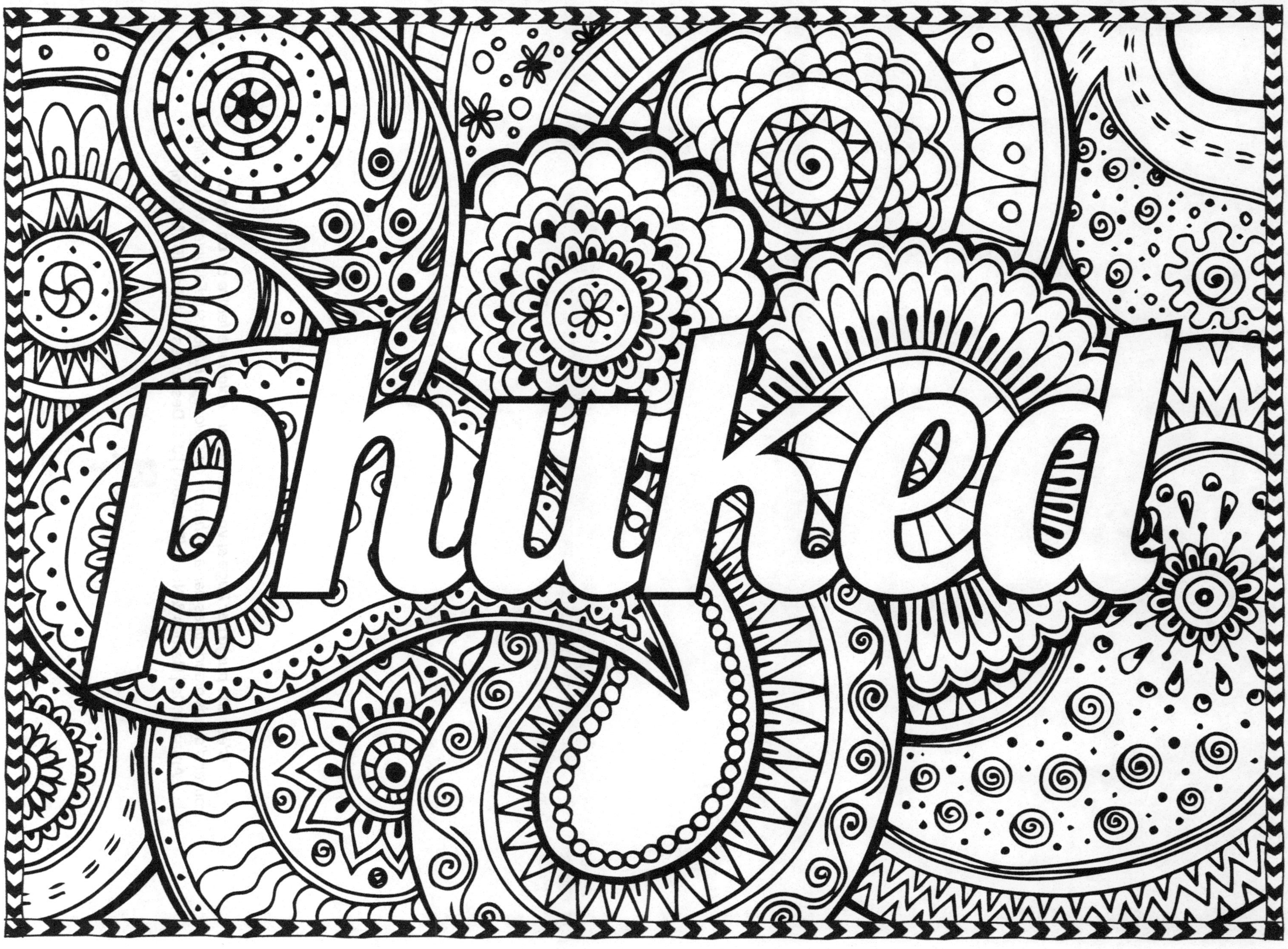
phuked

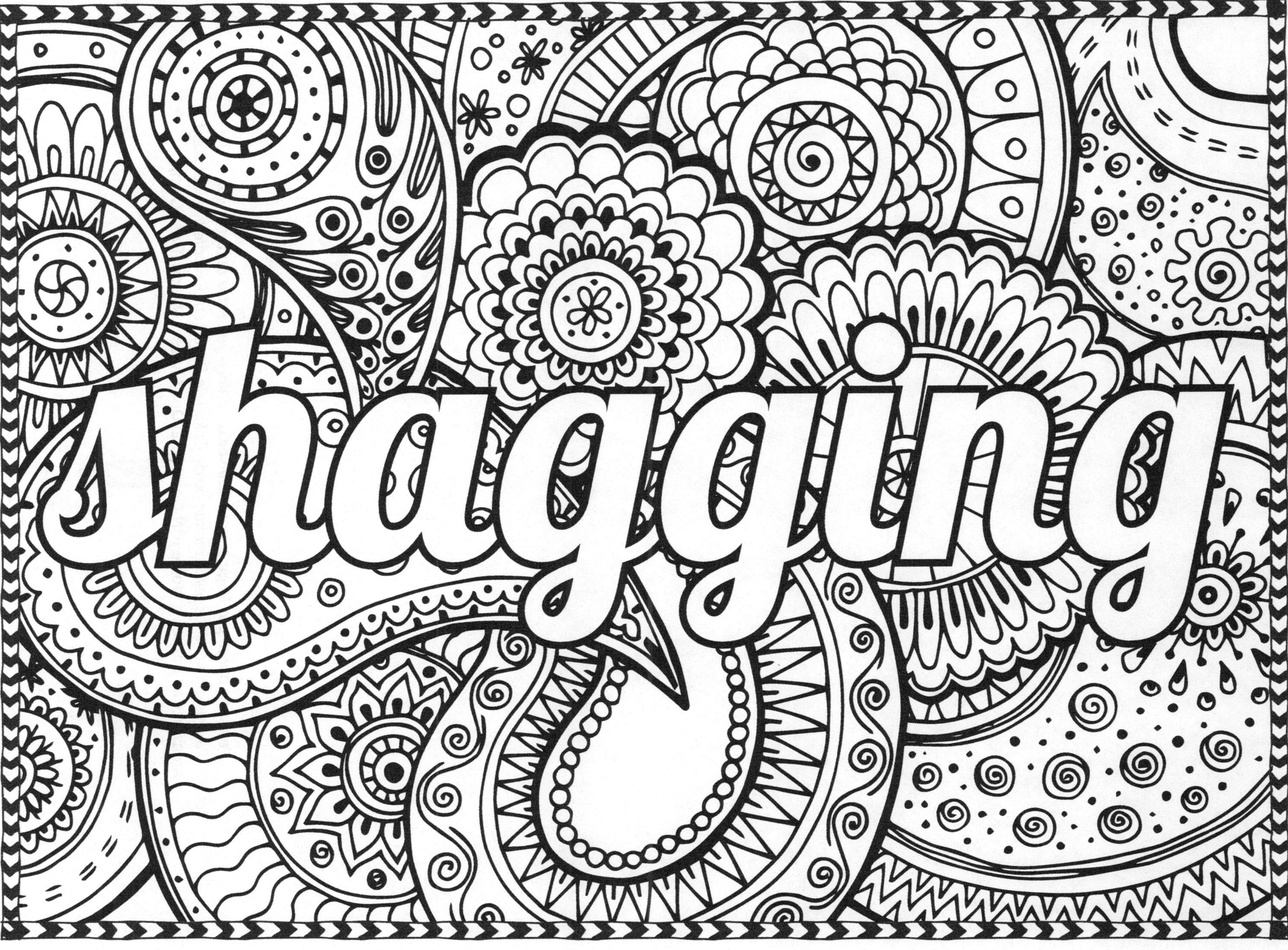
shagging

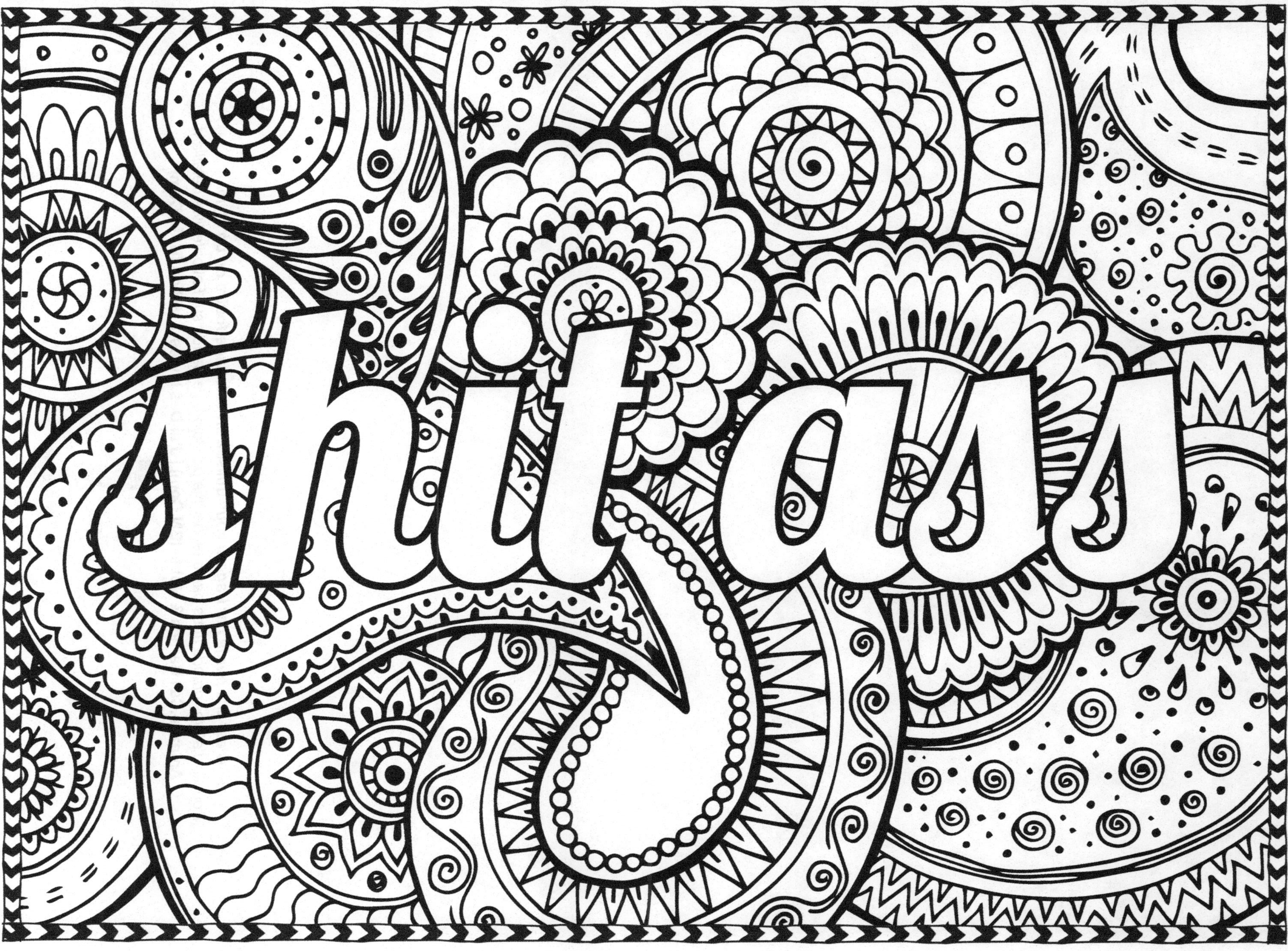
shit ass

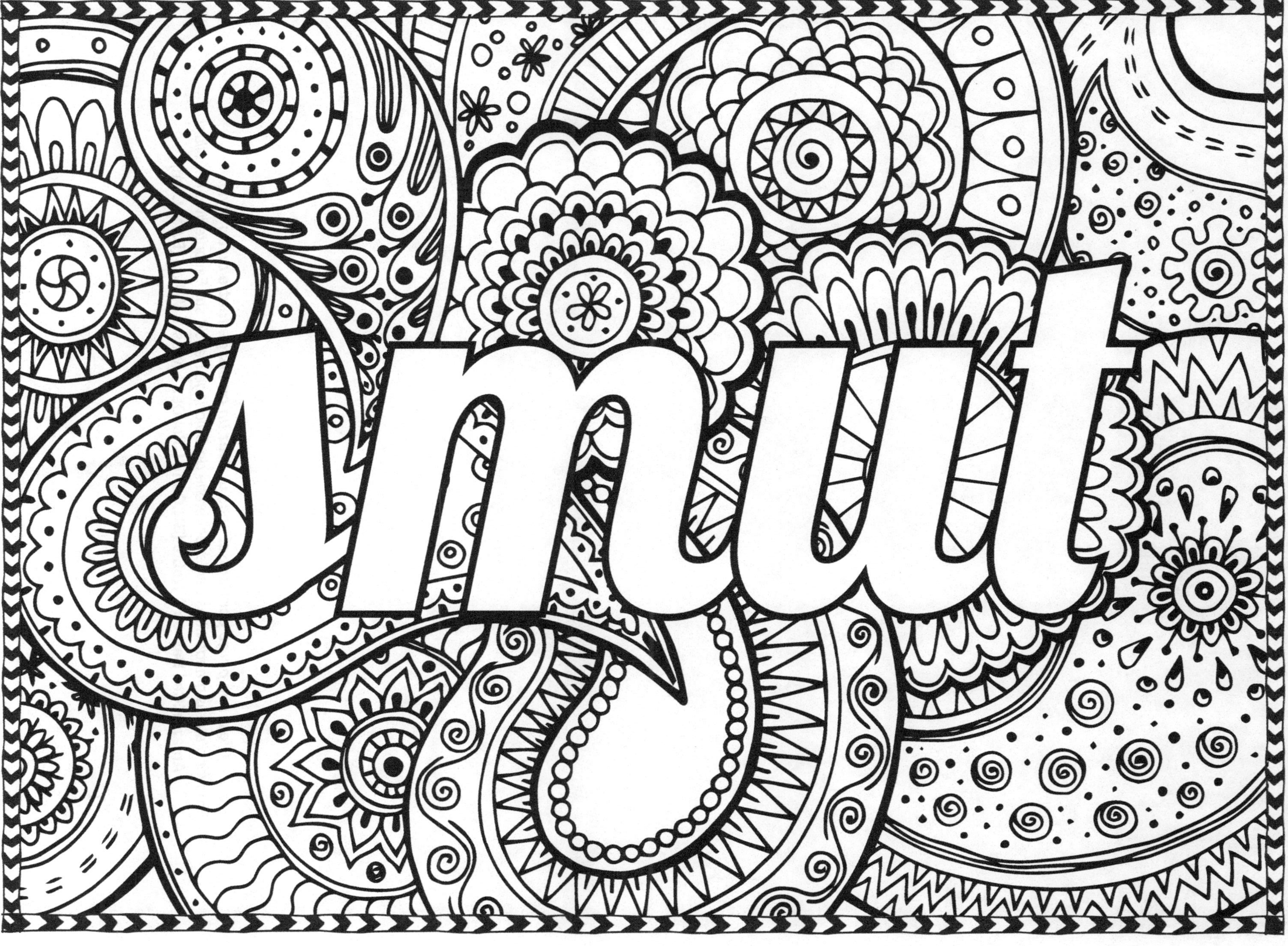
smut

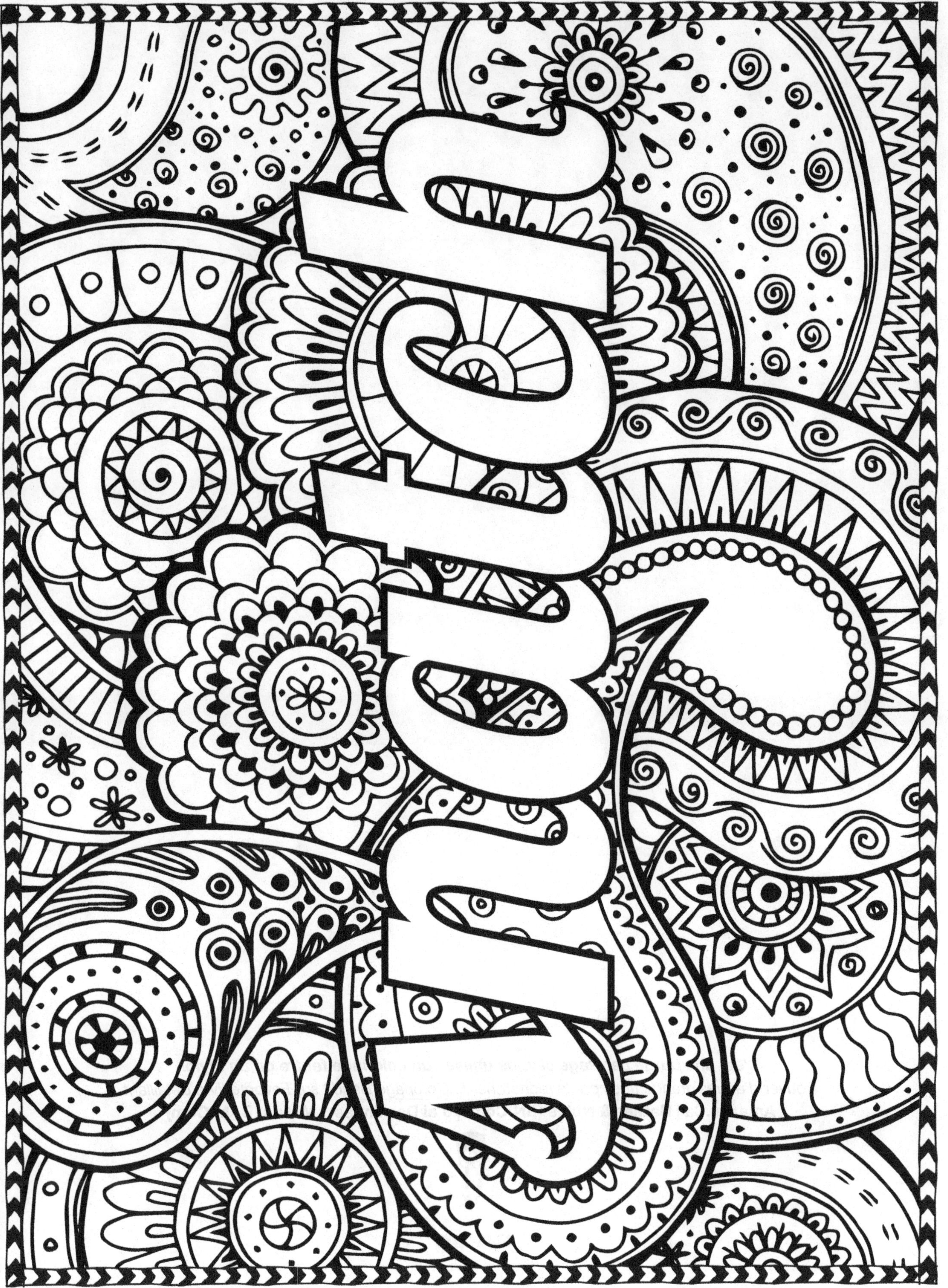
grateful

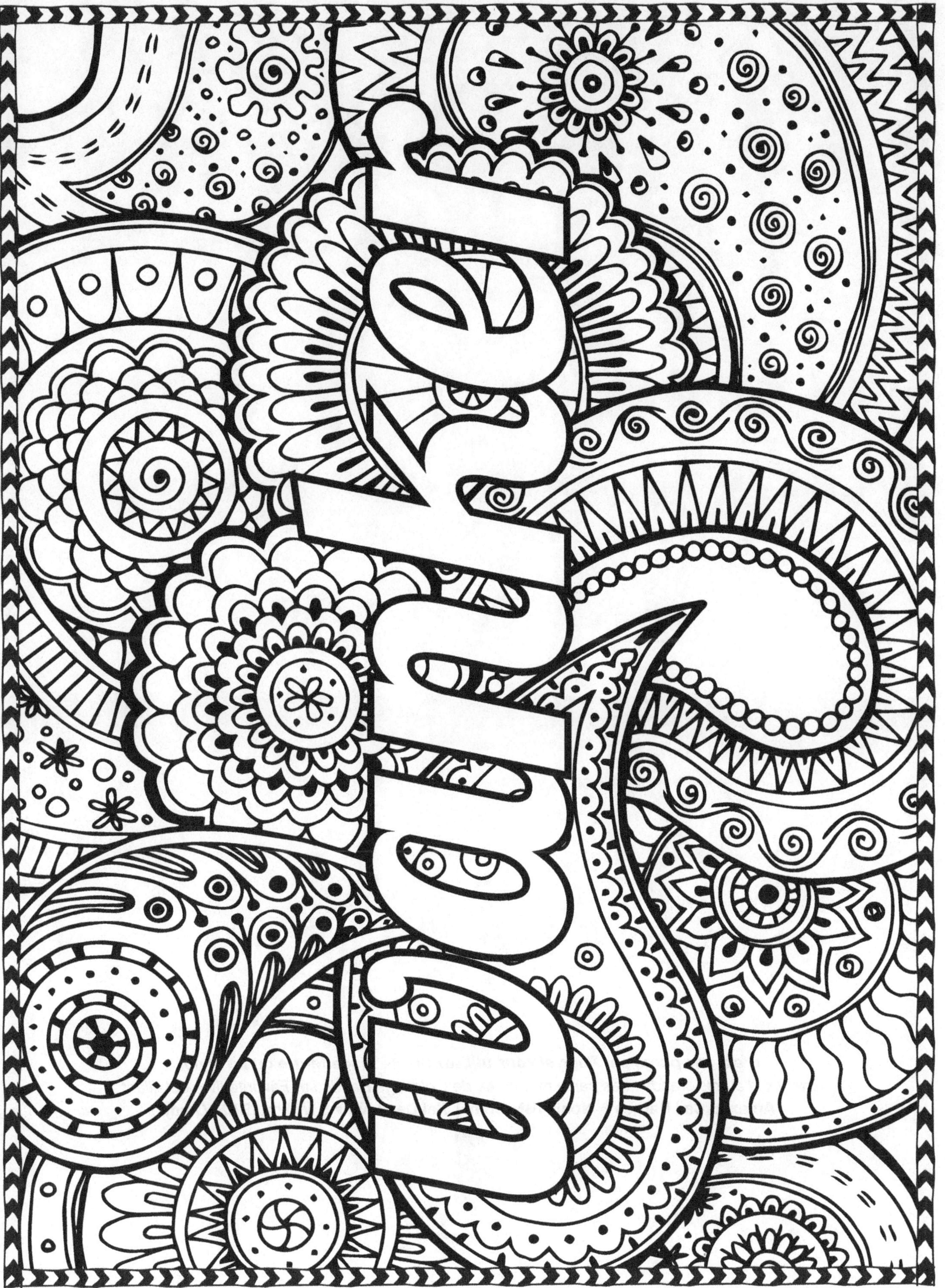
thankful

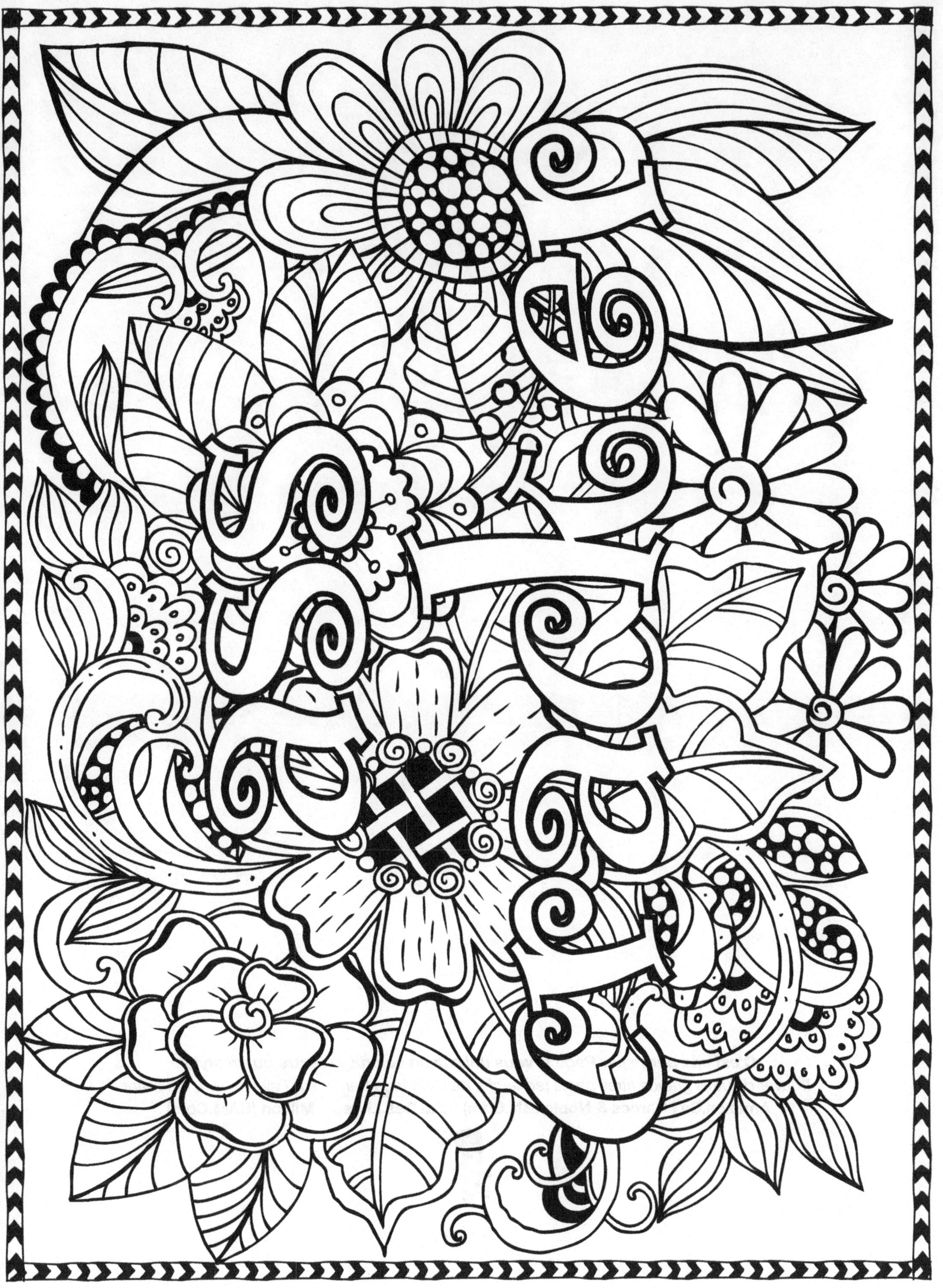

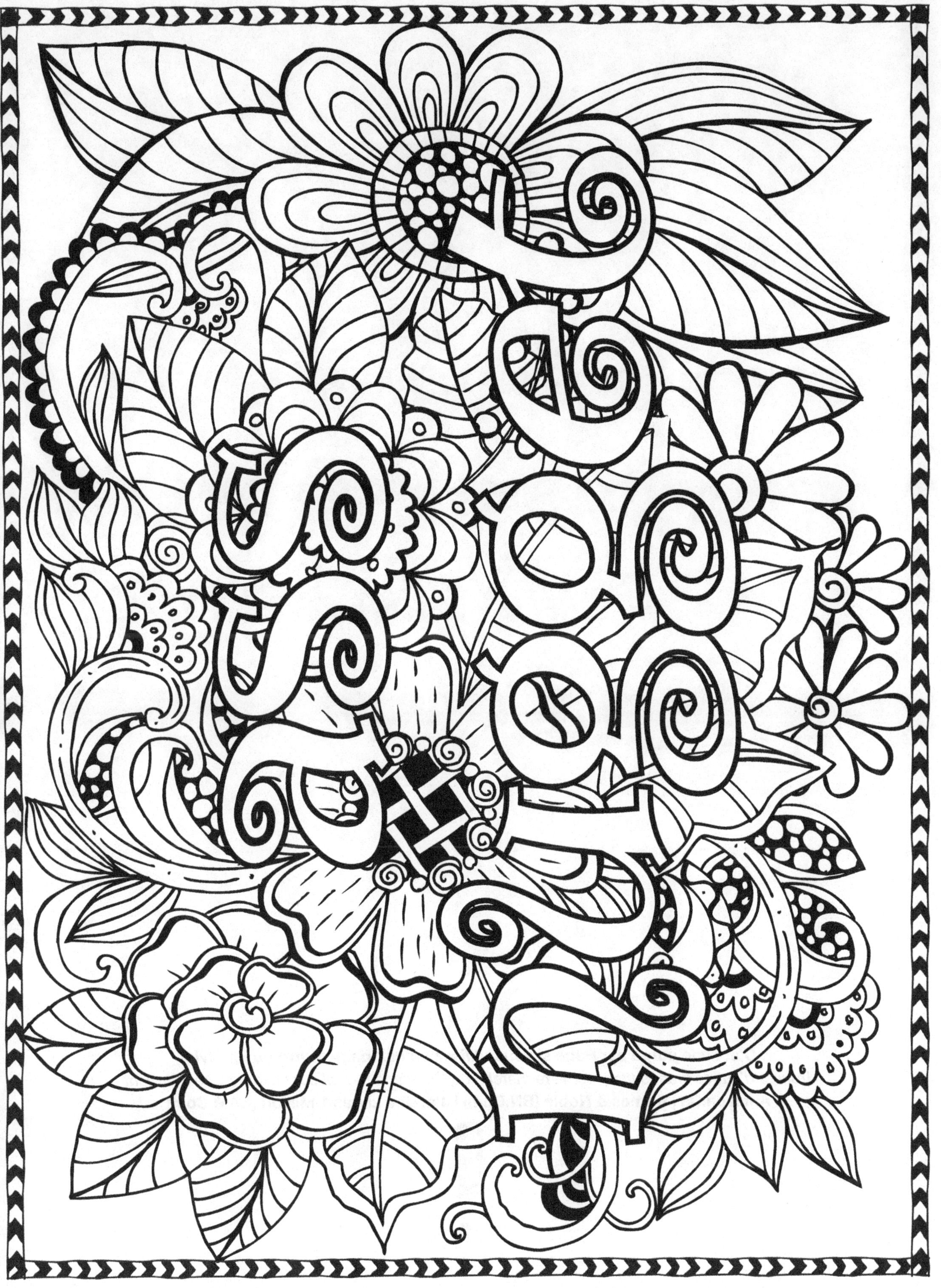

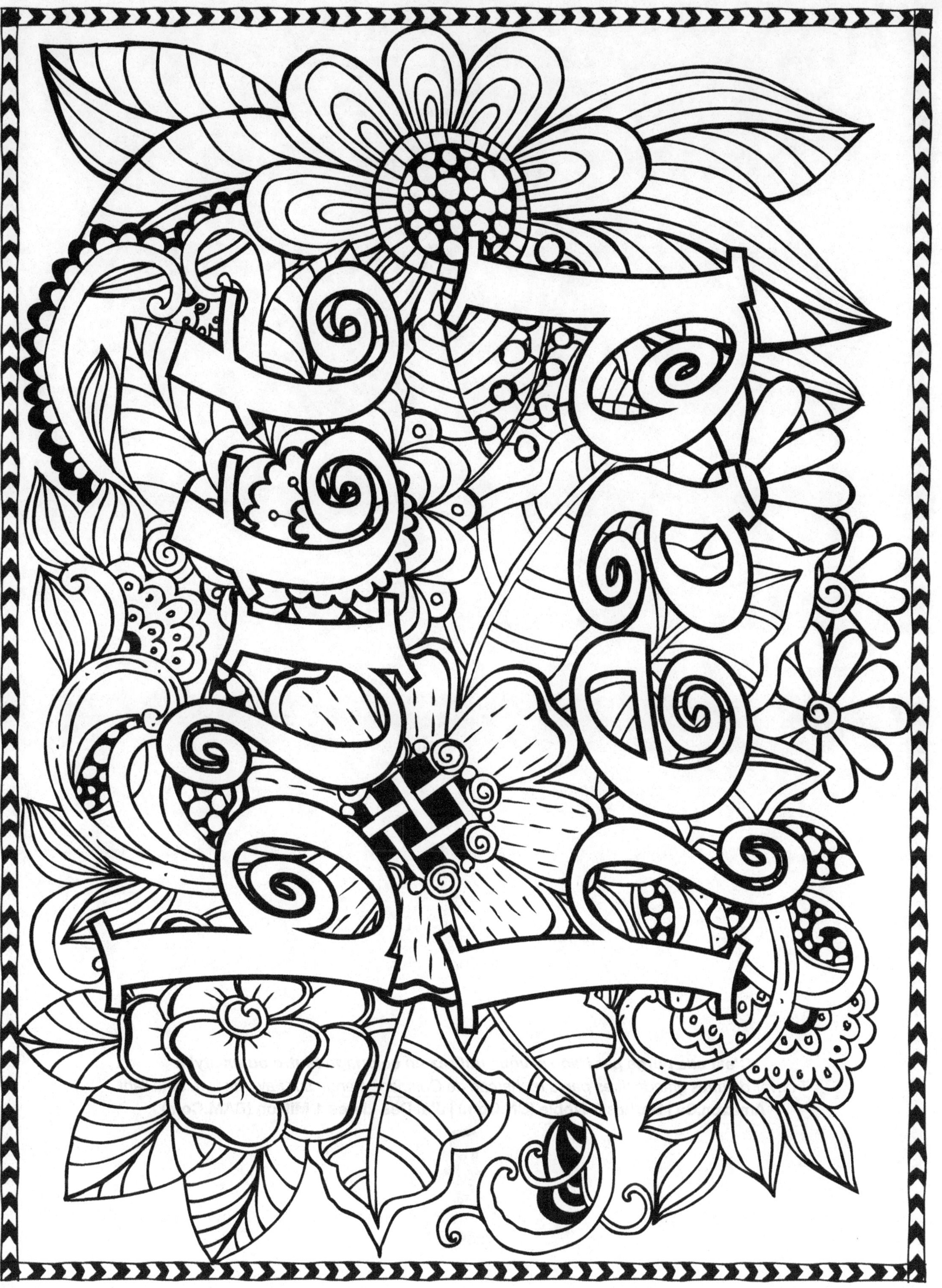

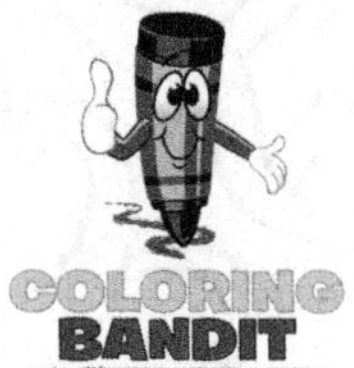

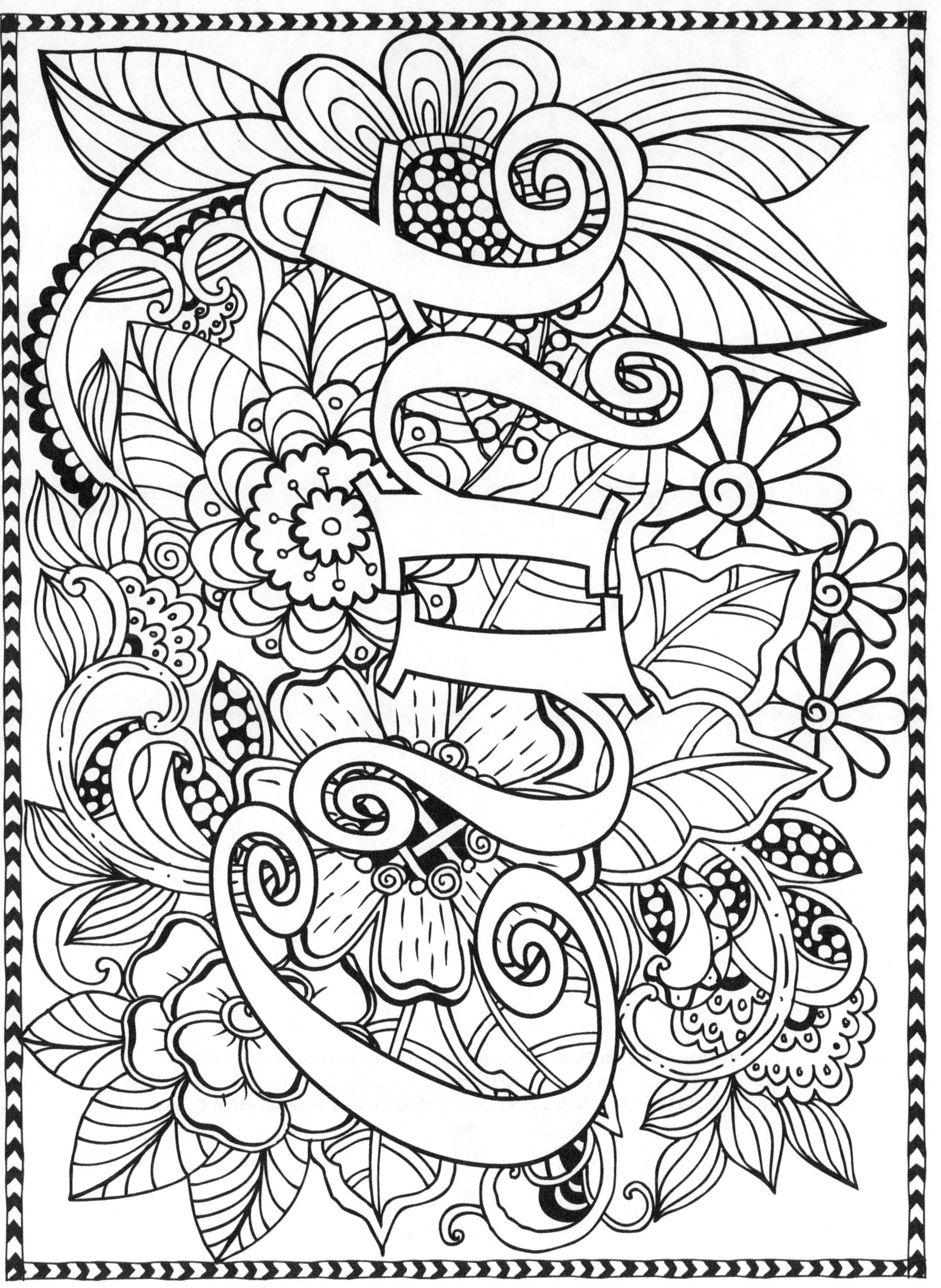

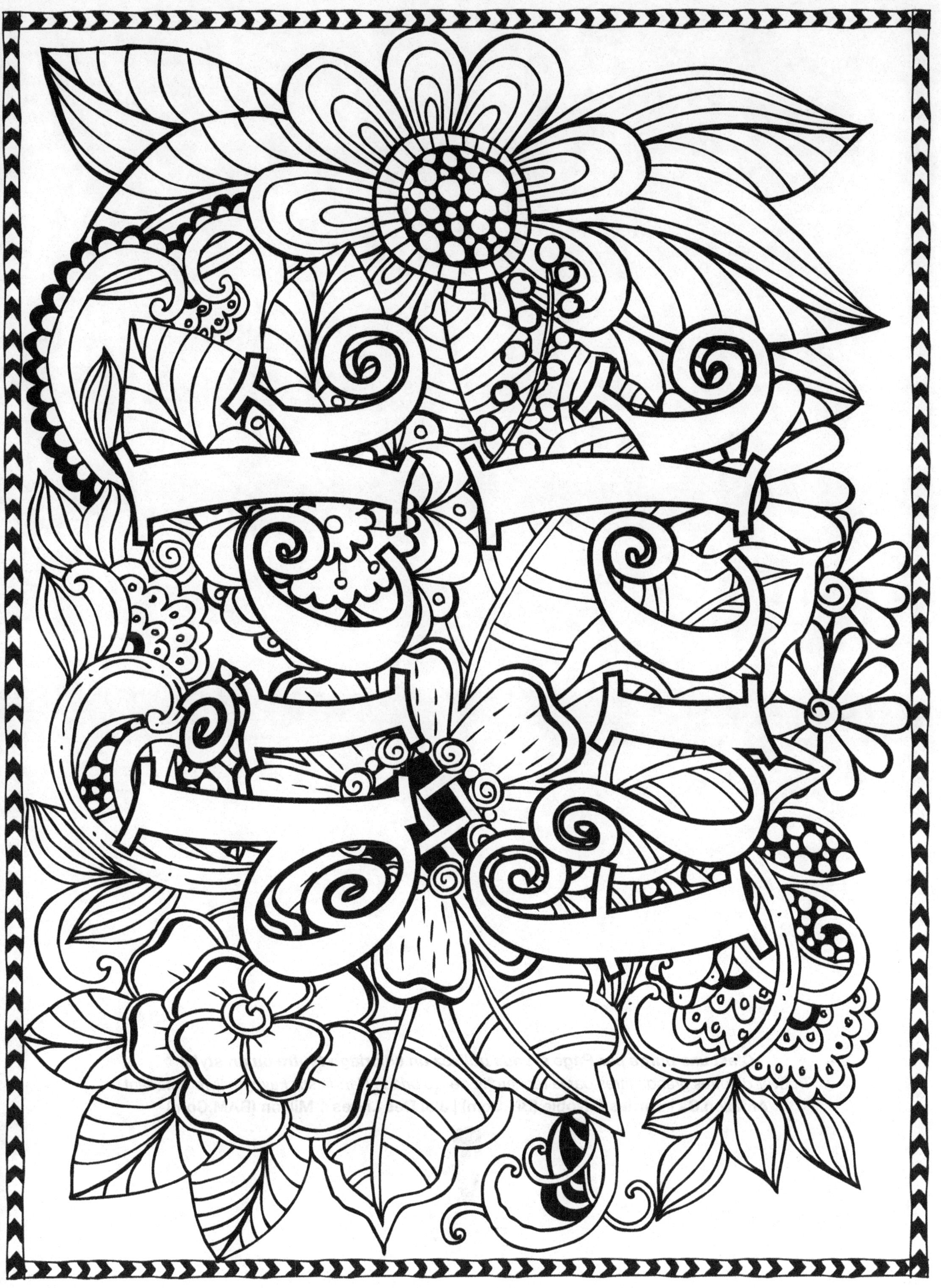

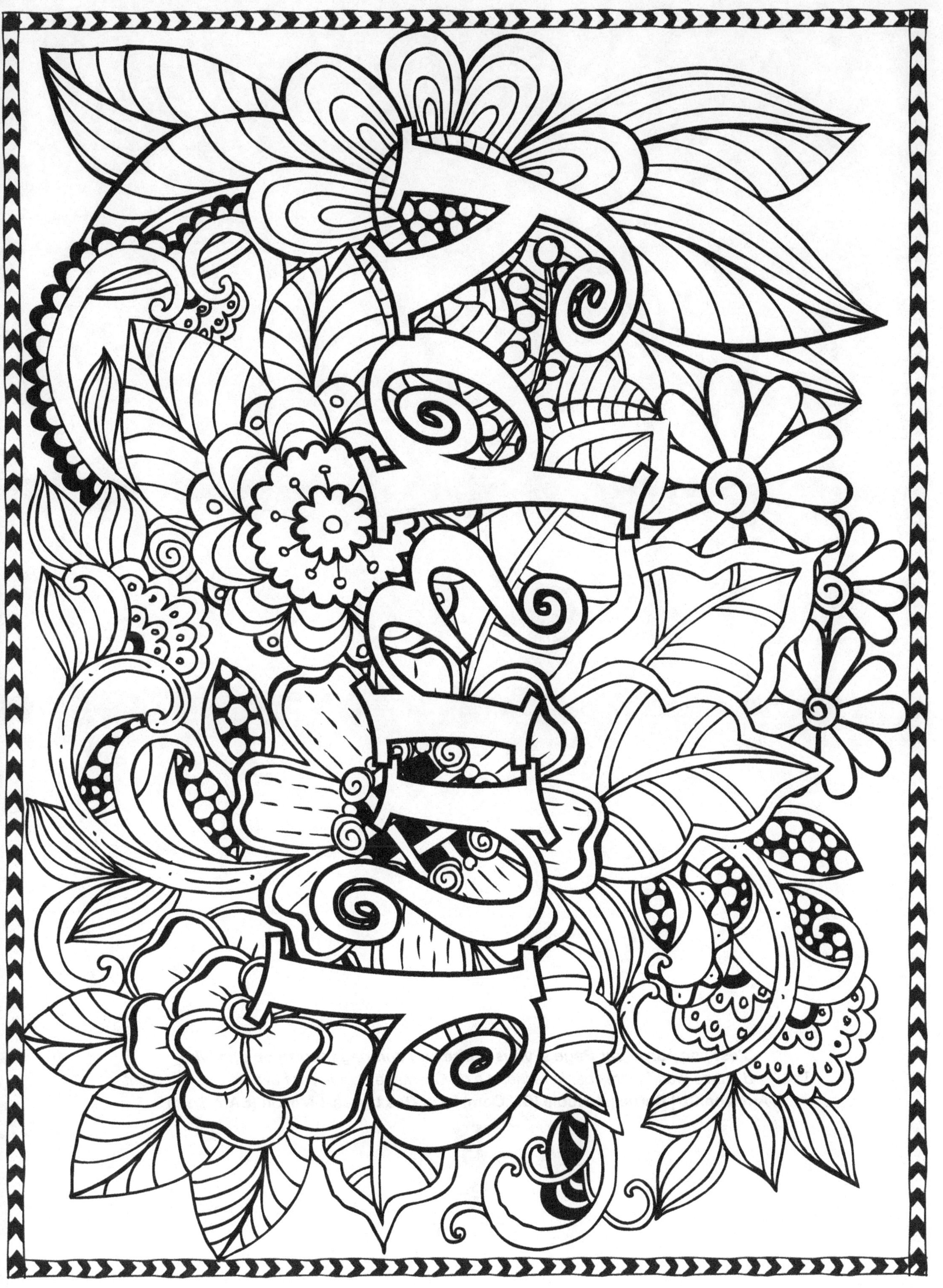

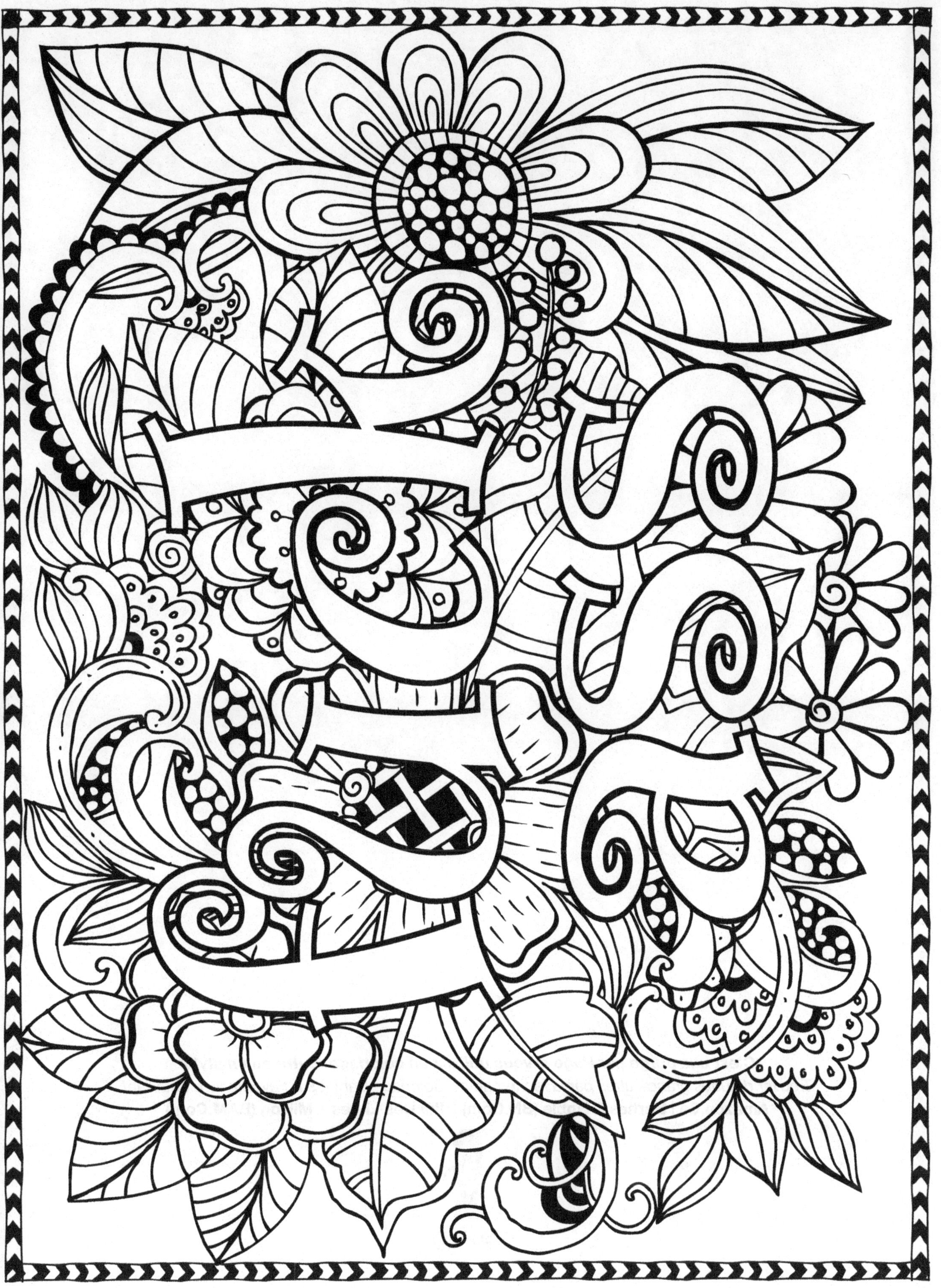

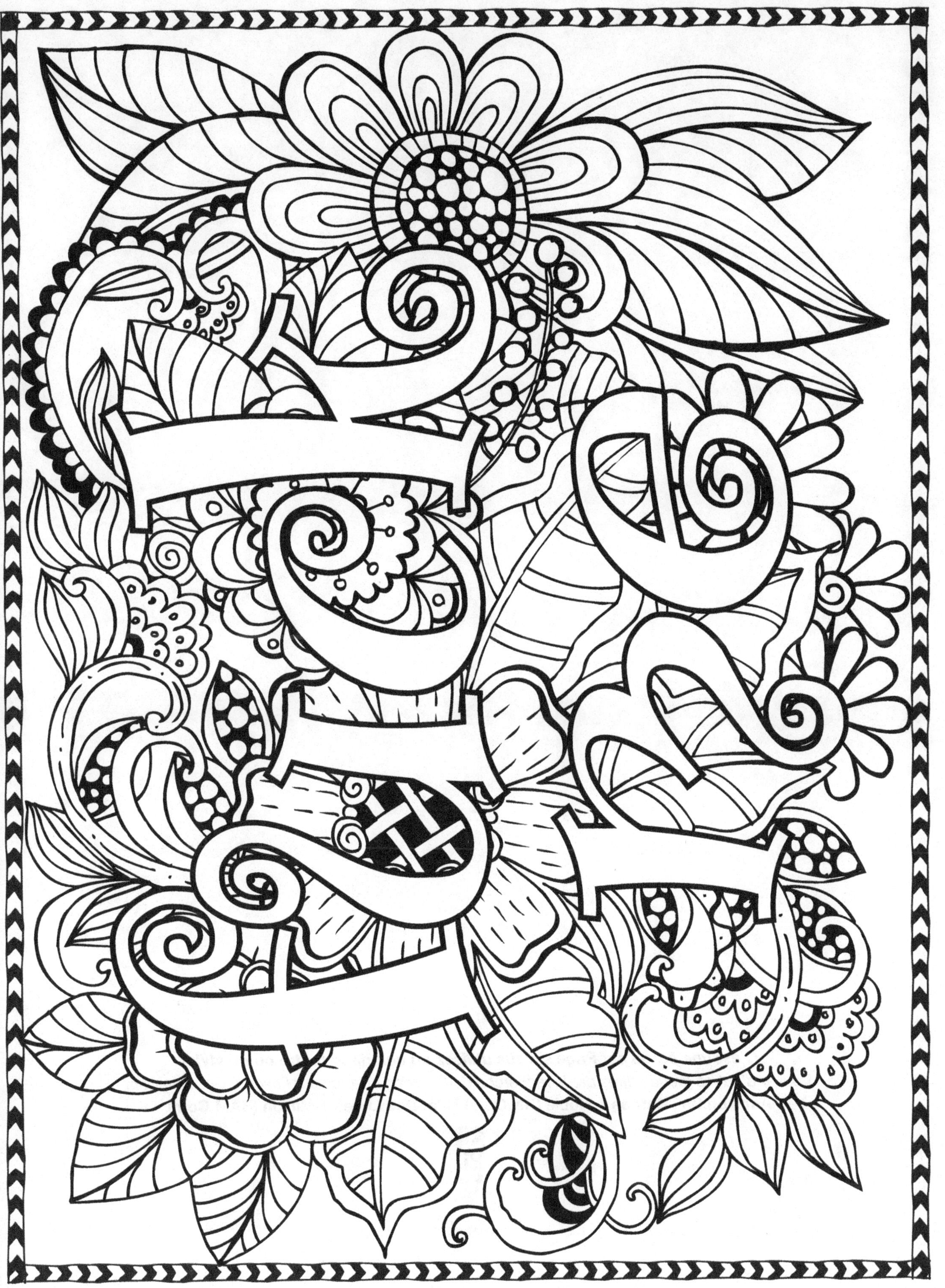

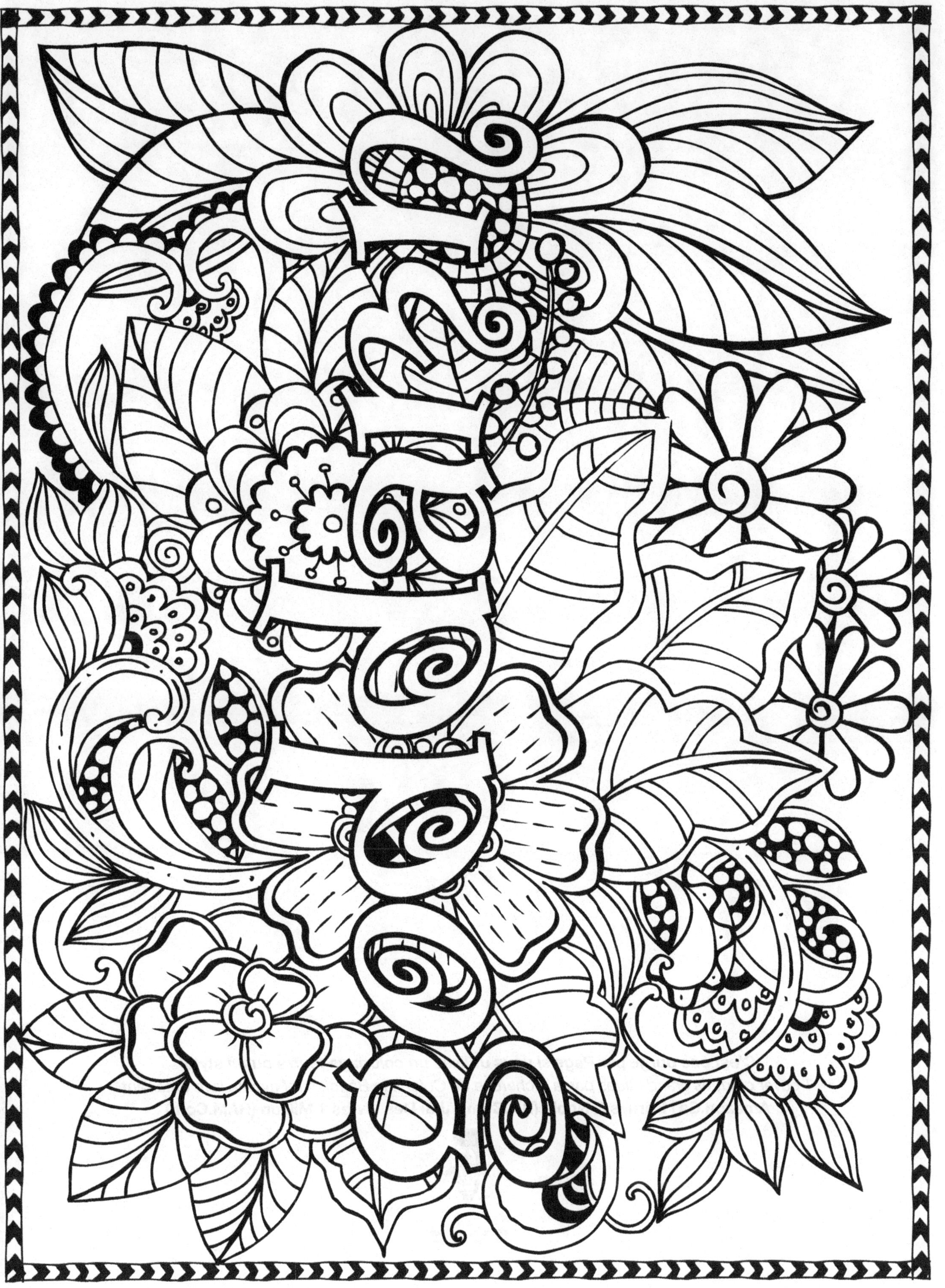

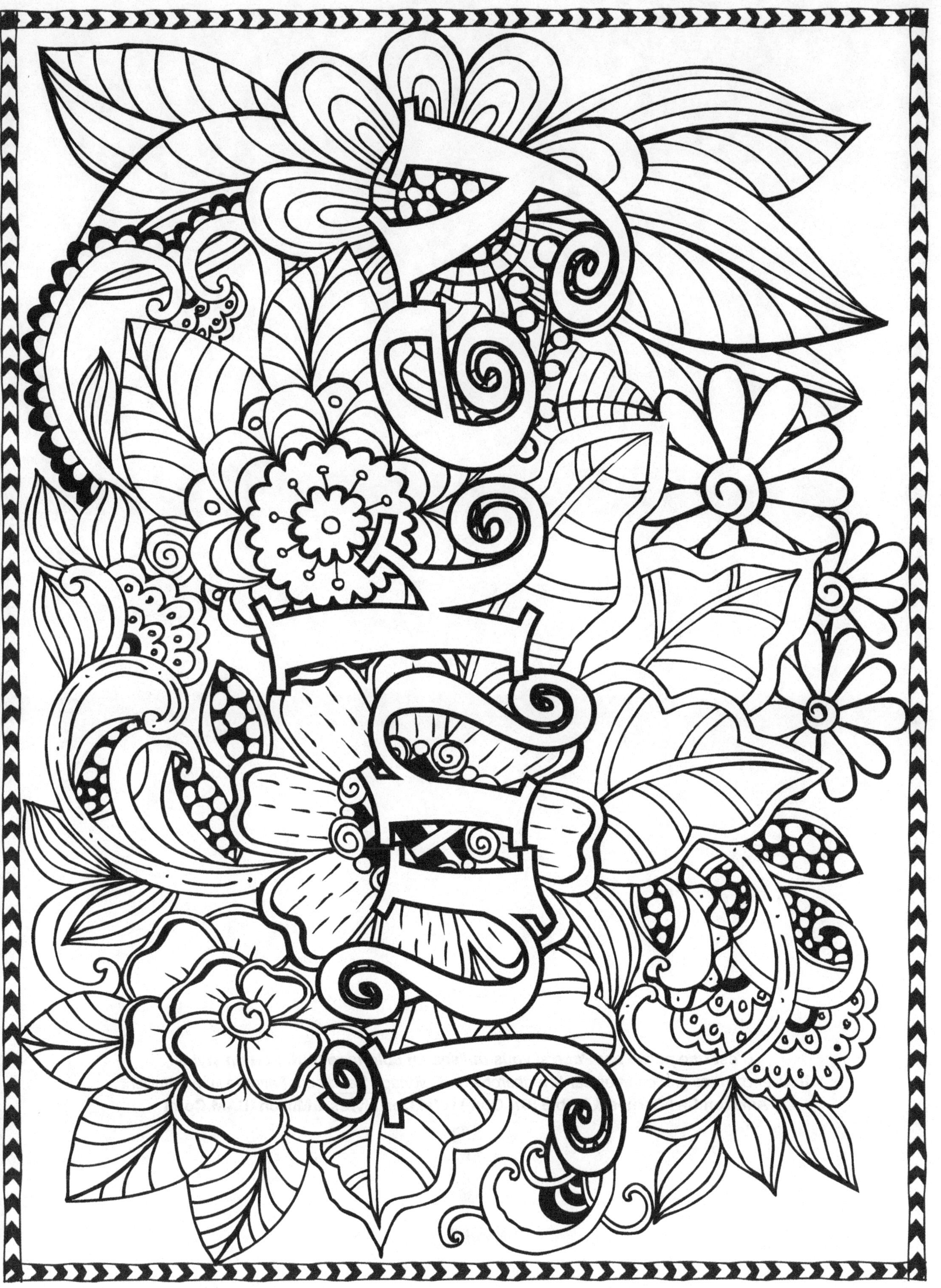

C'est une purge par Page si vous utilisez un coloriage feutre ou un stylo!

Trouver d'autres grands titres par la recherche de Coloriage Bandit sur Favorite livre détaillant

Amazon.Ca | Barnes & Noble (BN.Com) | J'ai Des Livres 1 Million (BAM.Com)

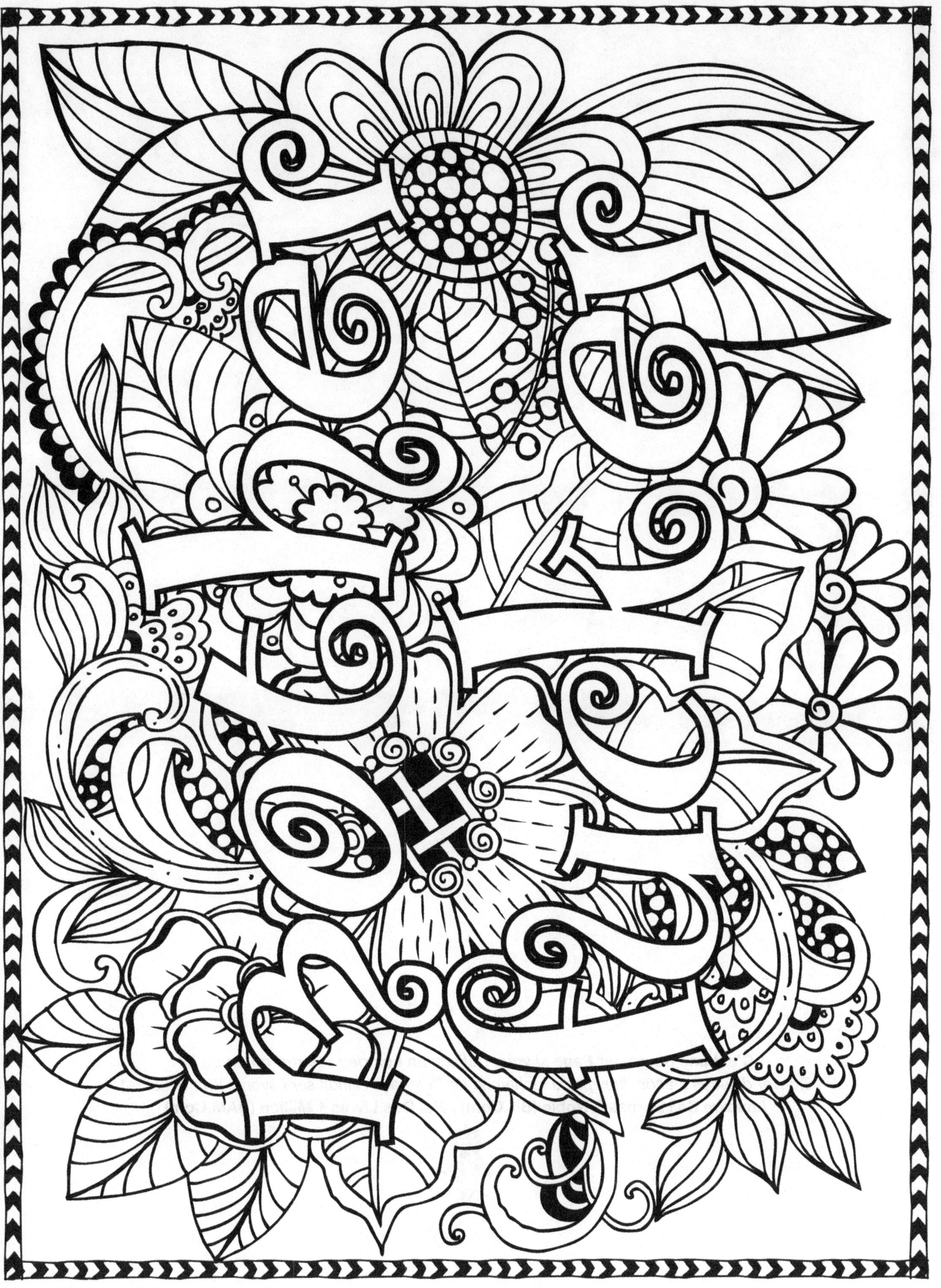

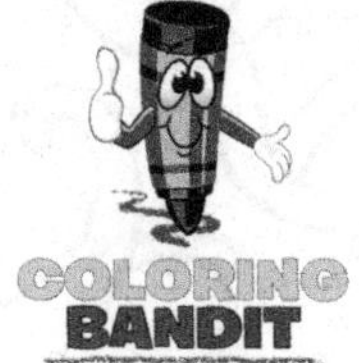
COLORING
BANDIT

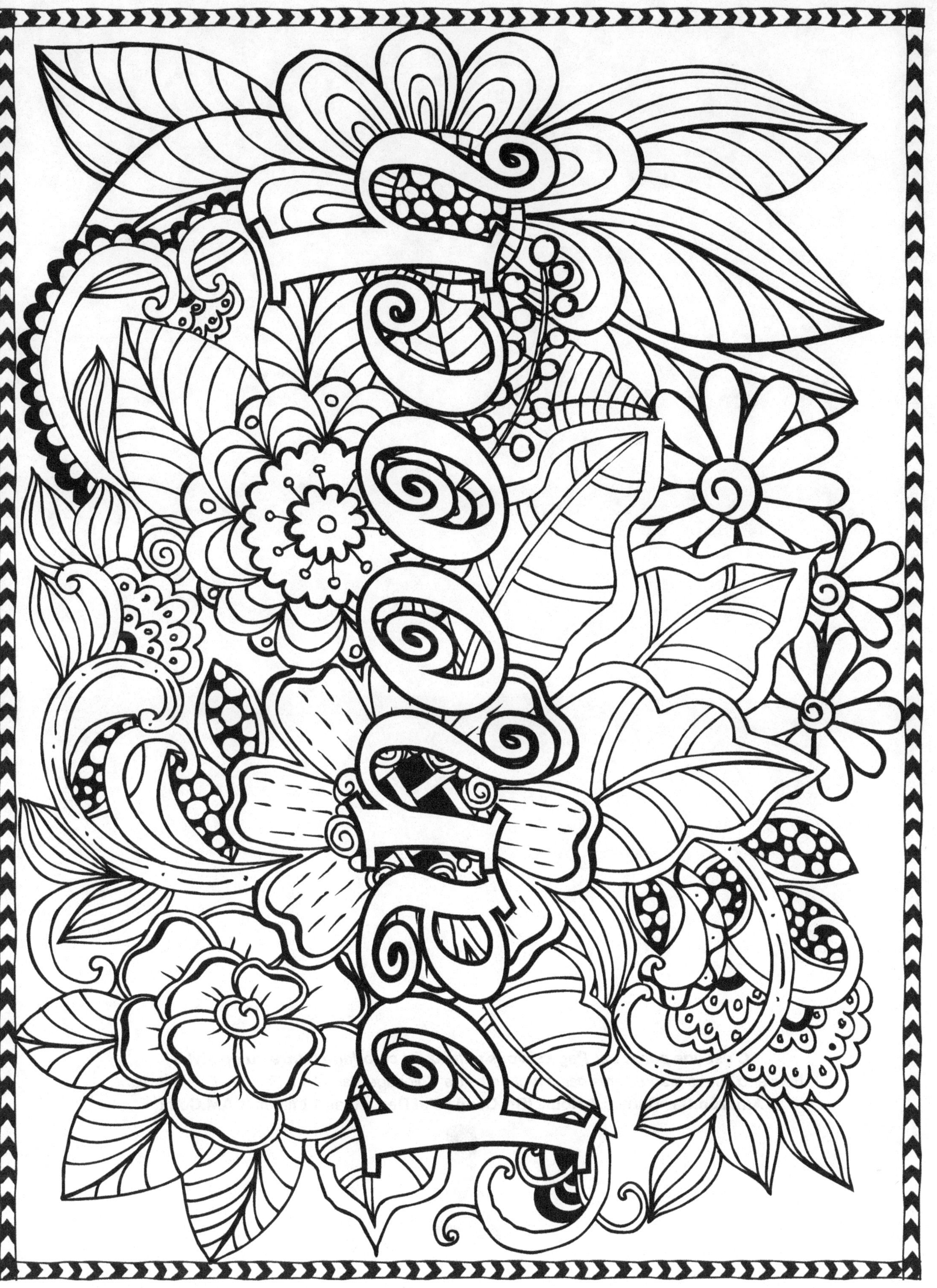

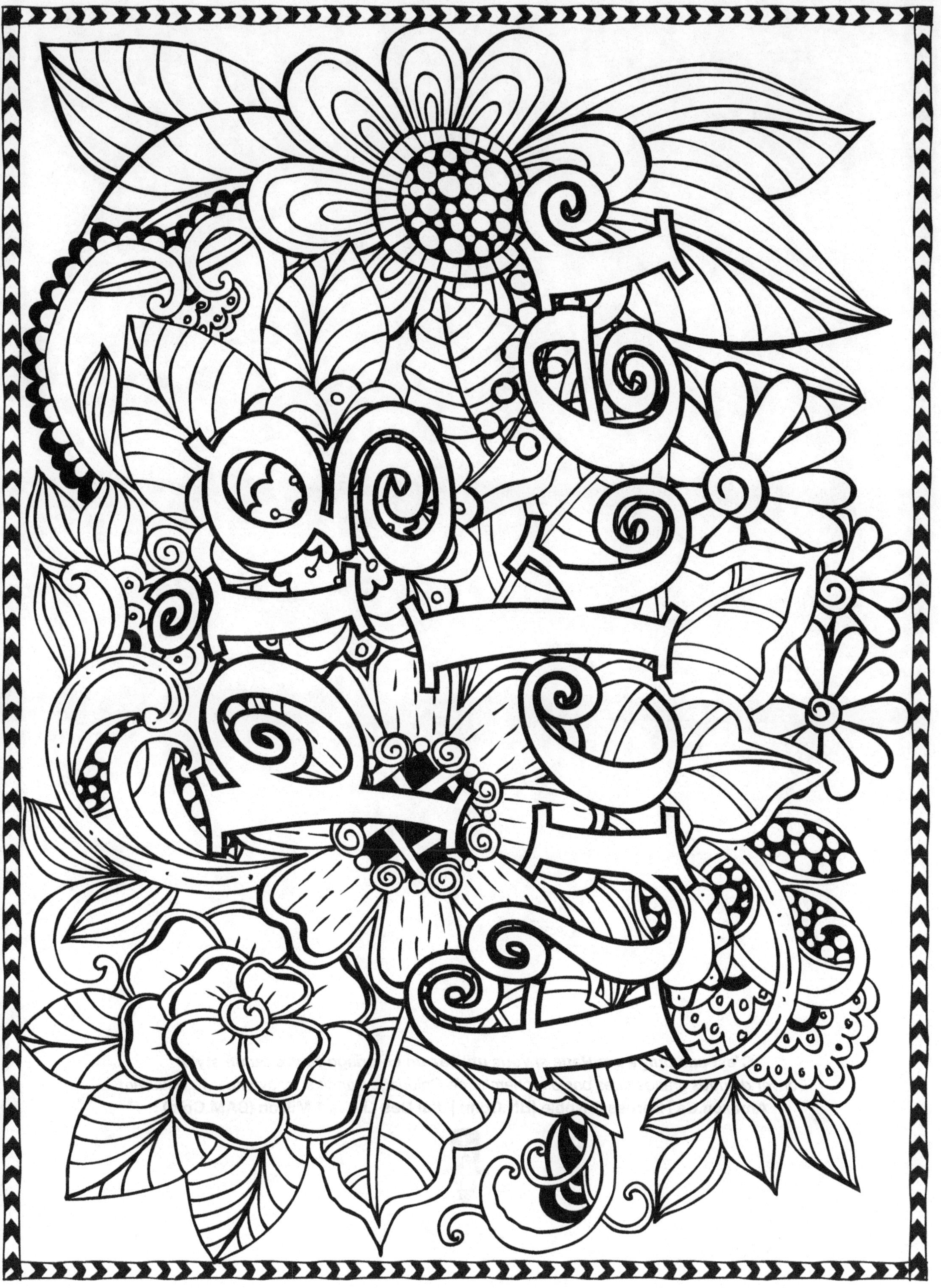

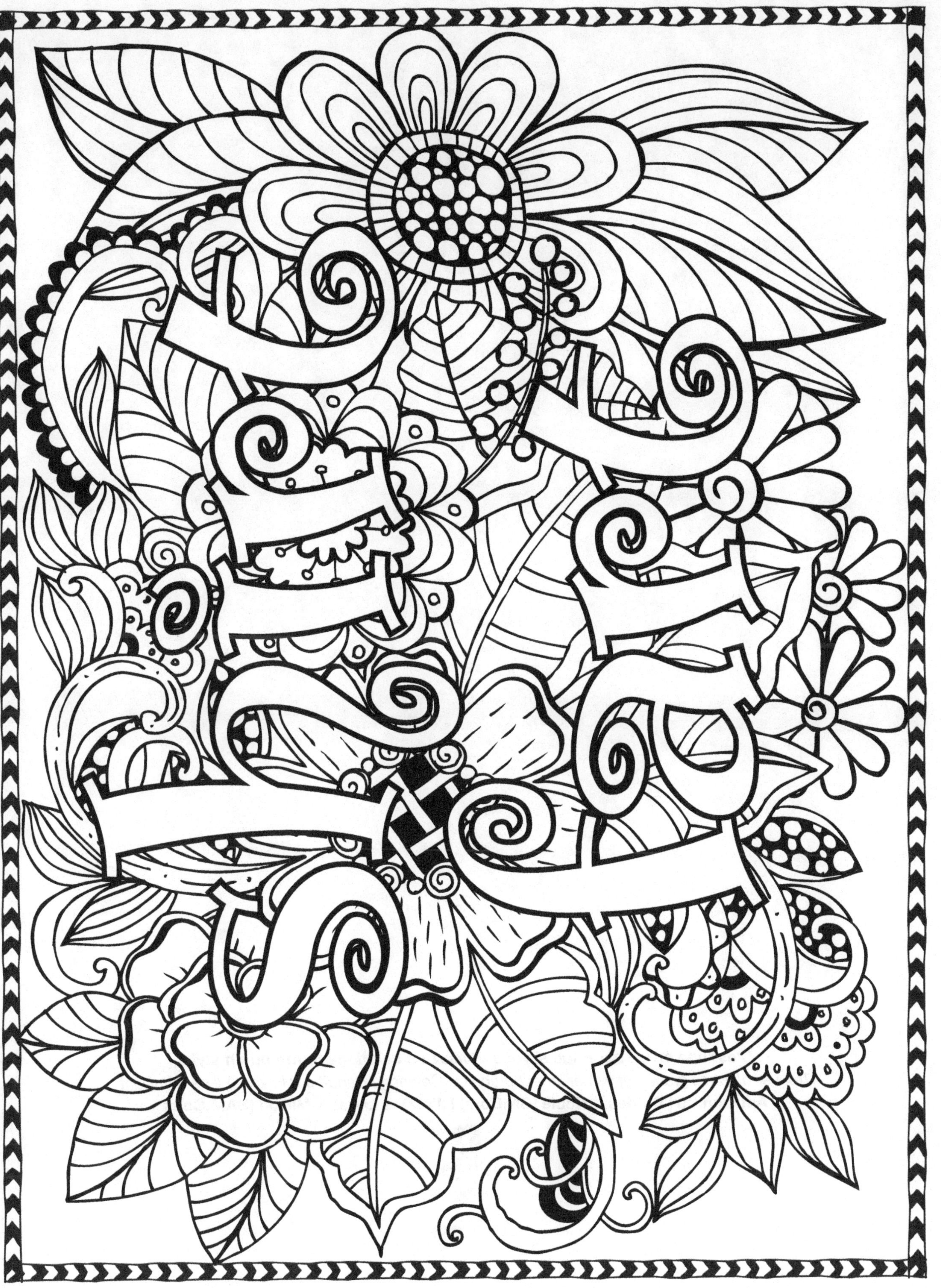

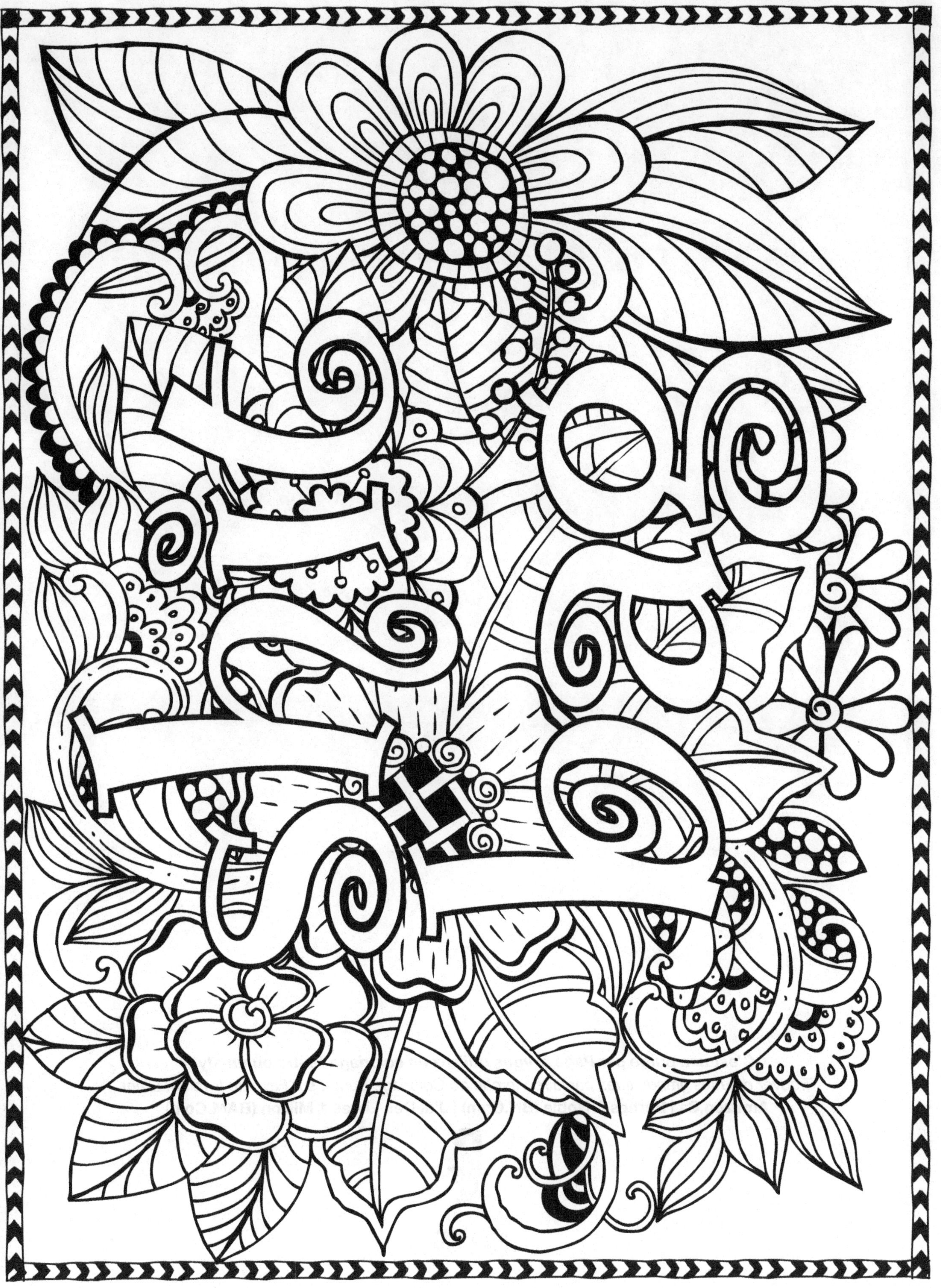

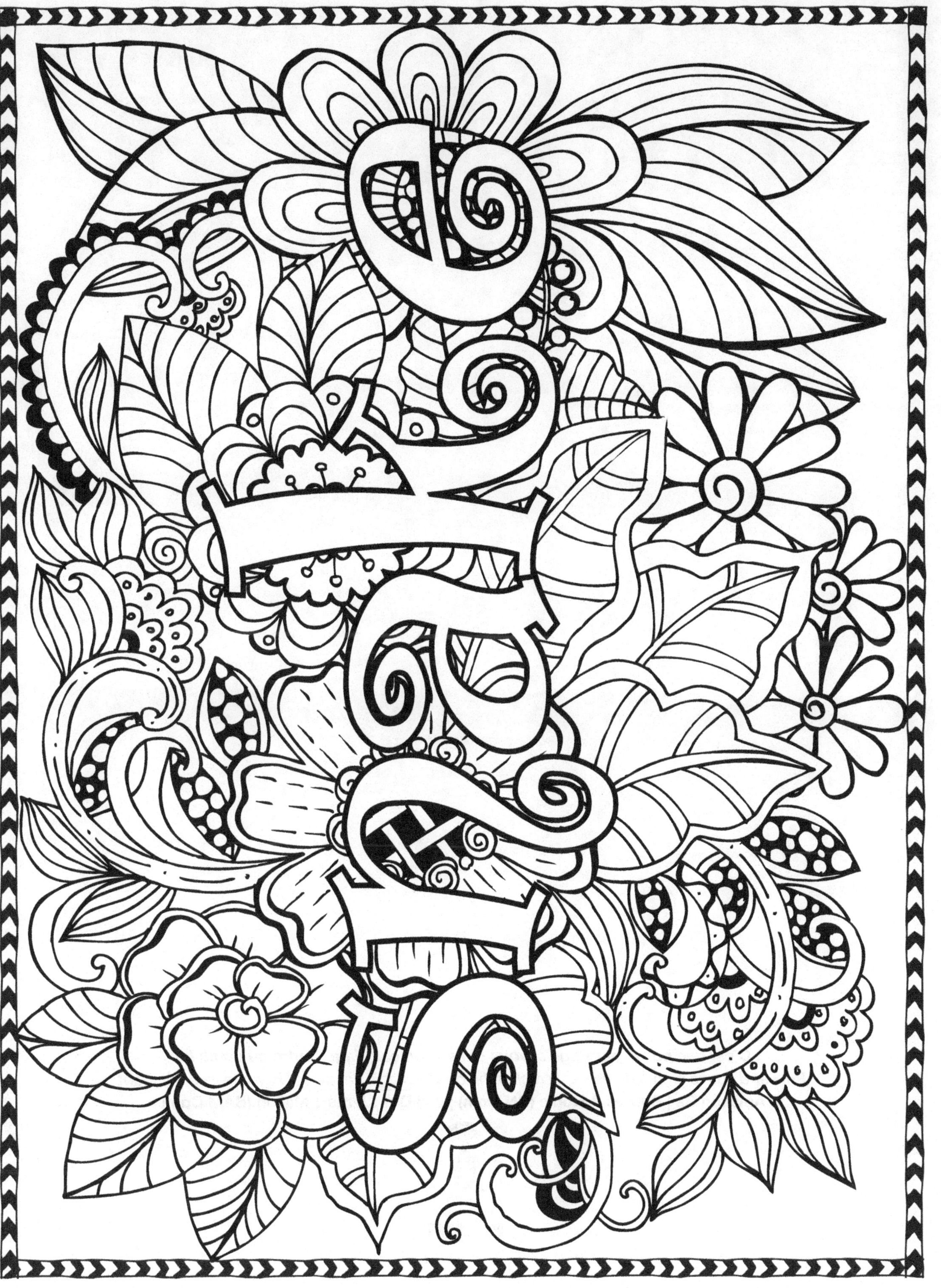

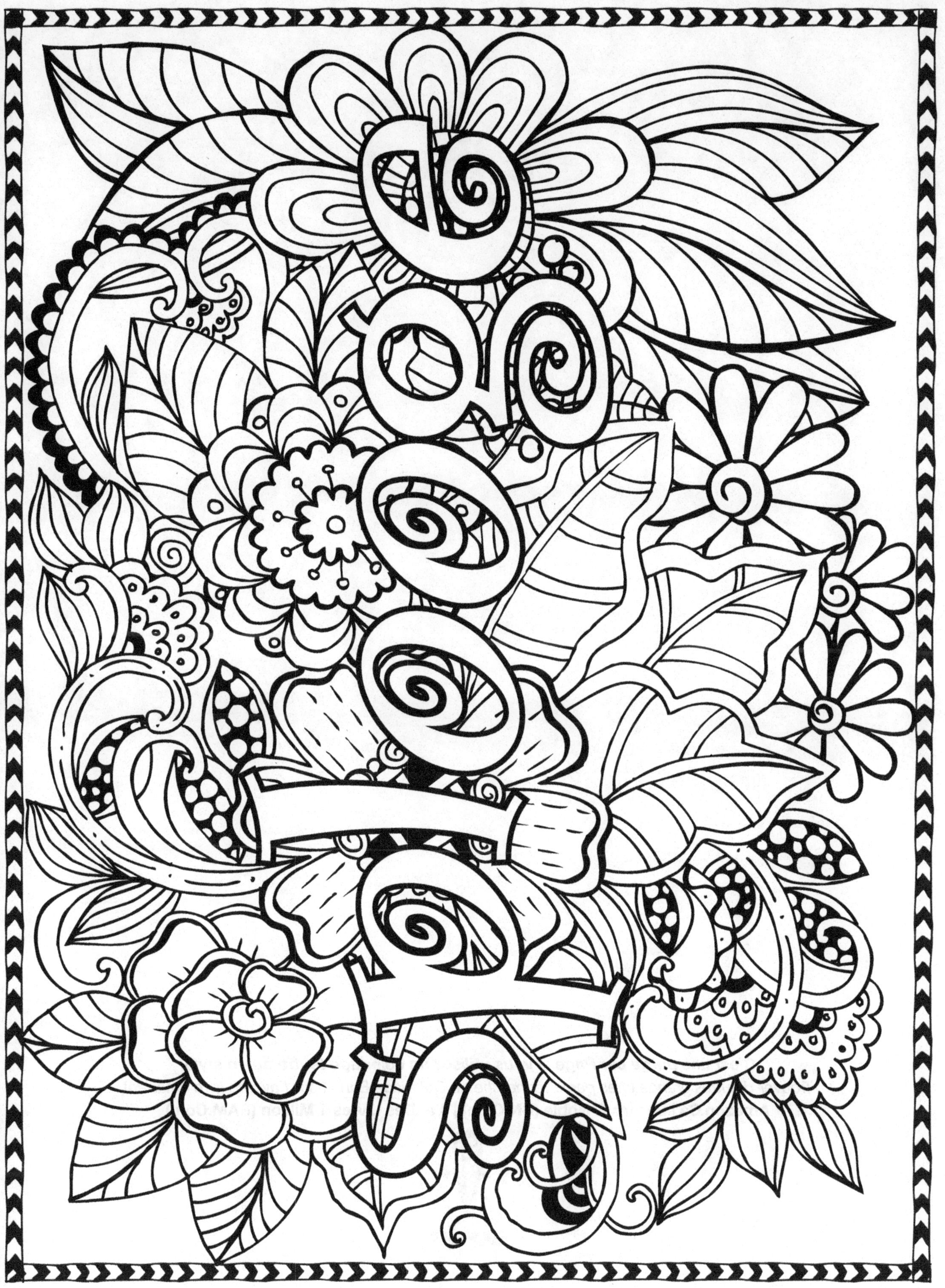

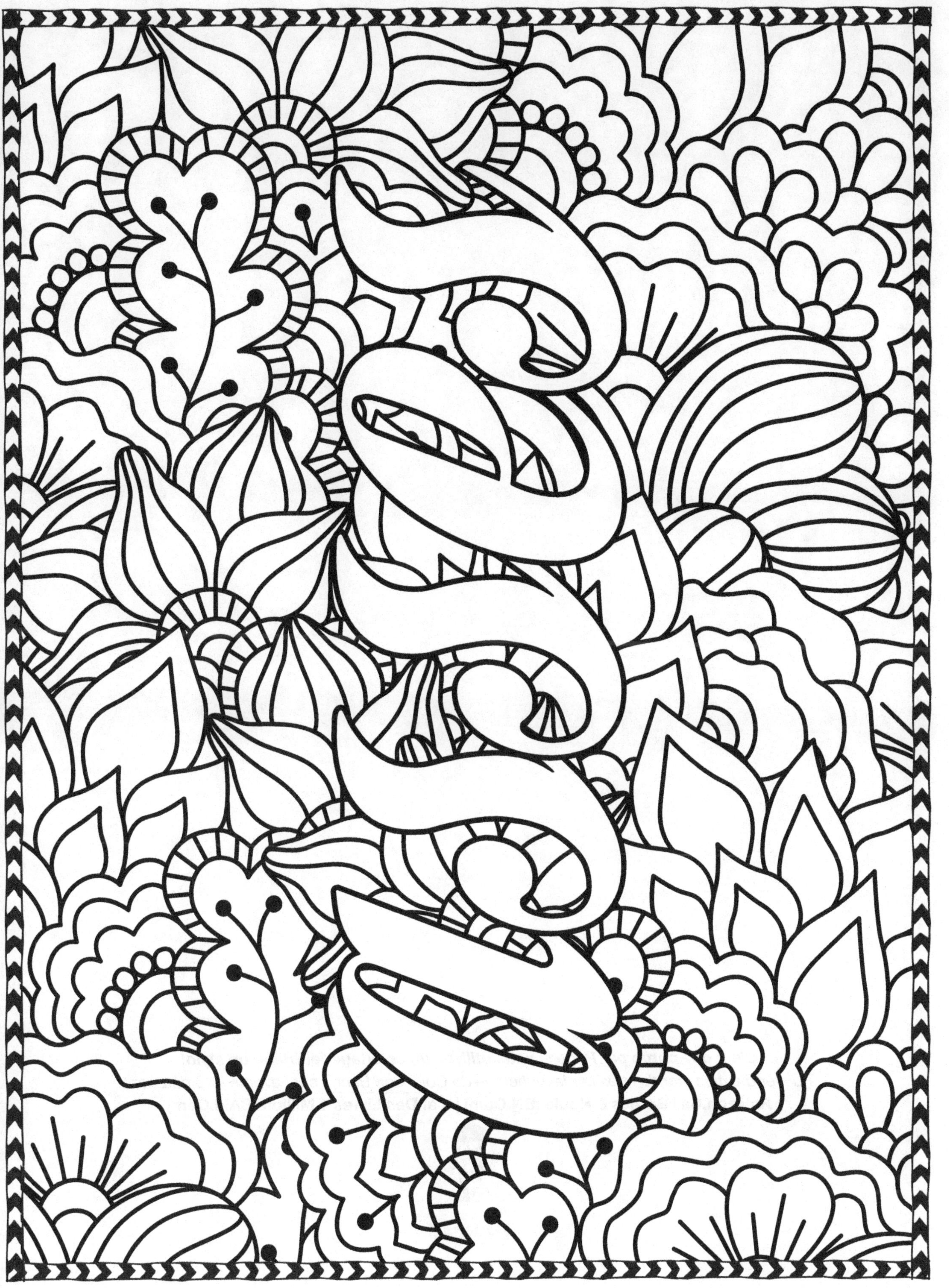

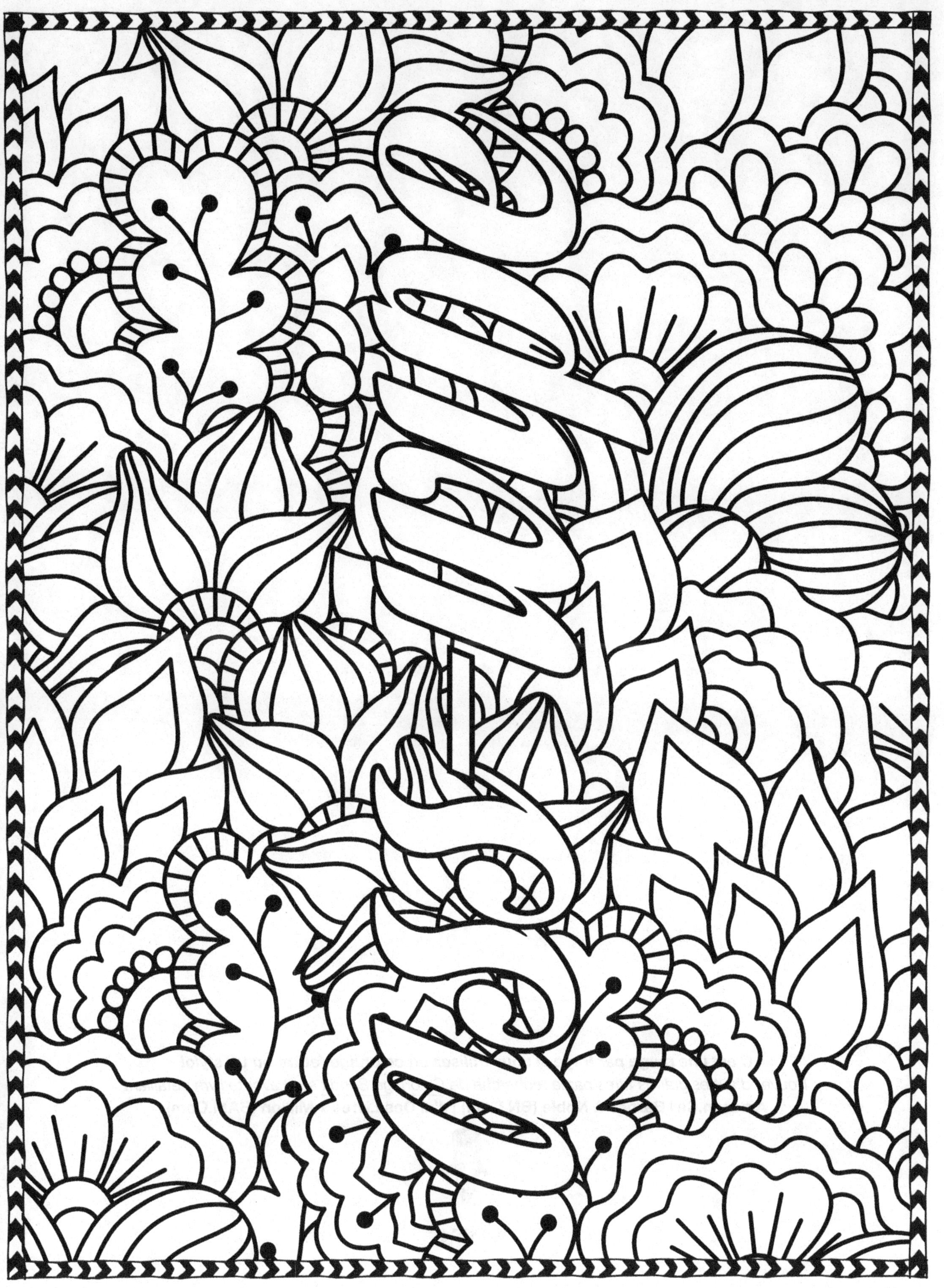

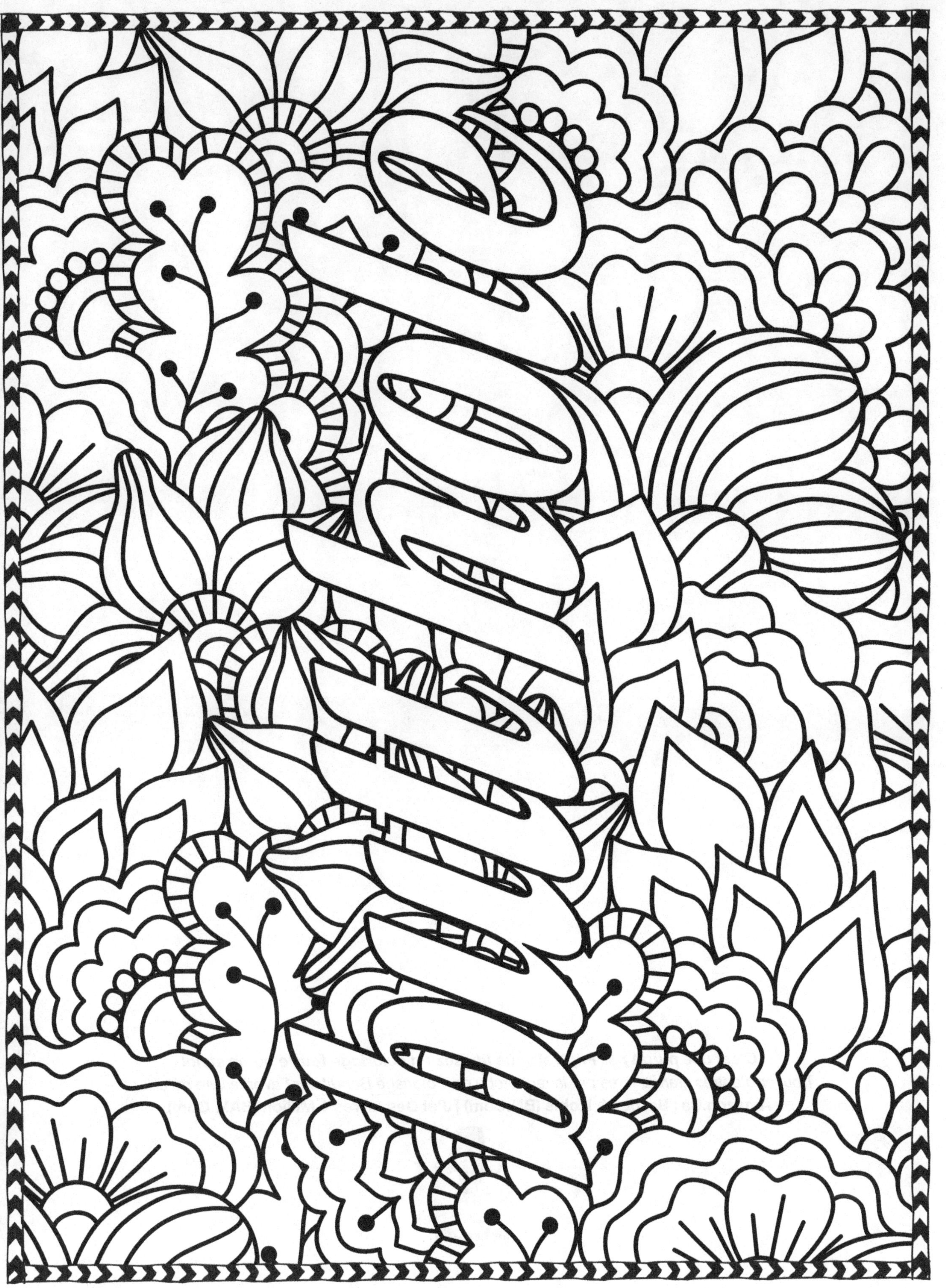

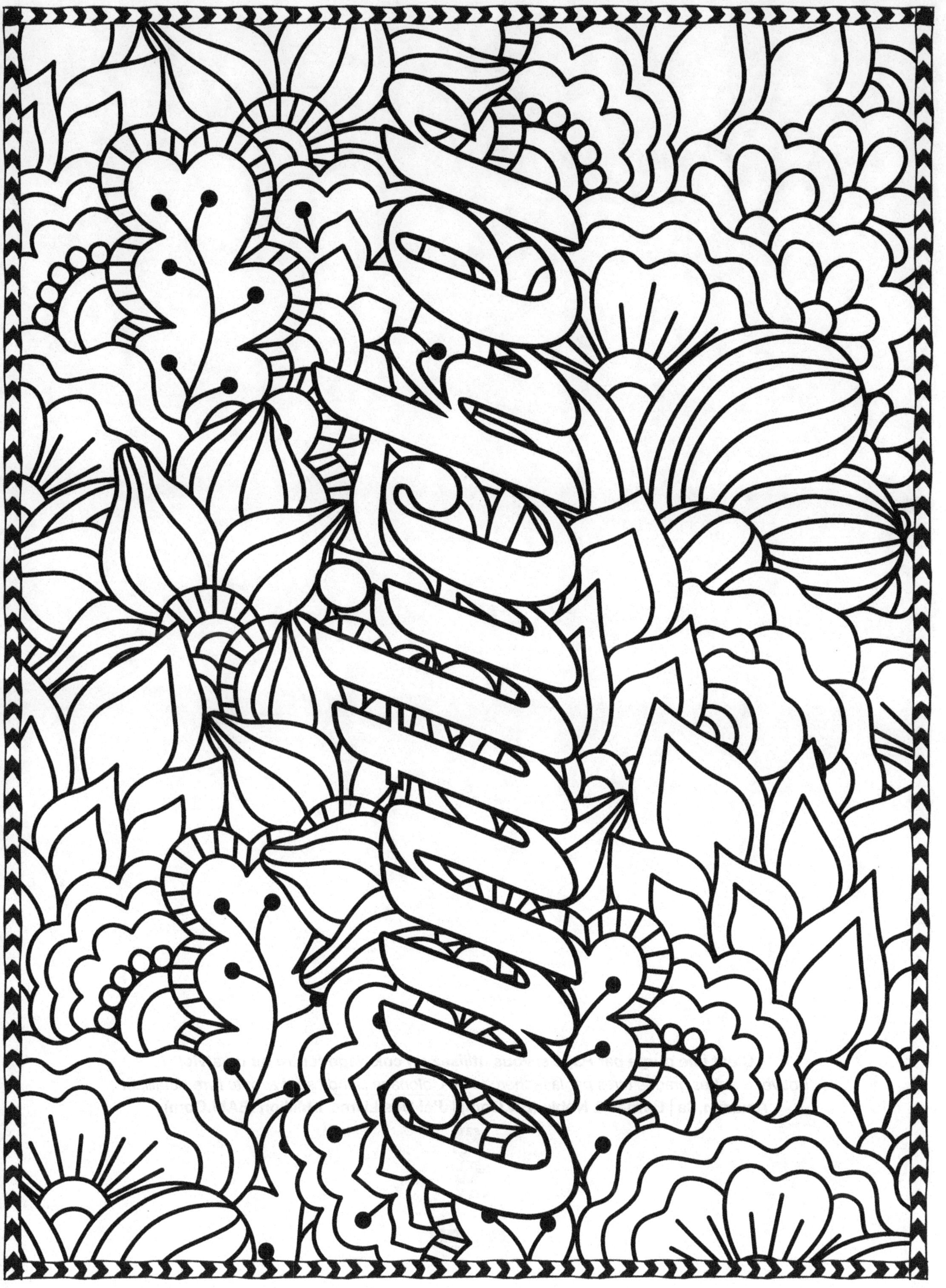

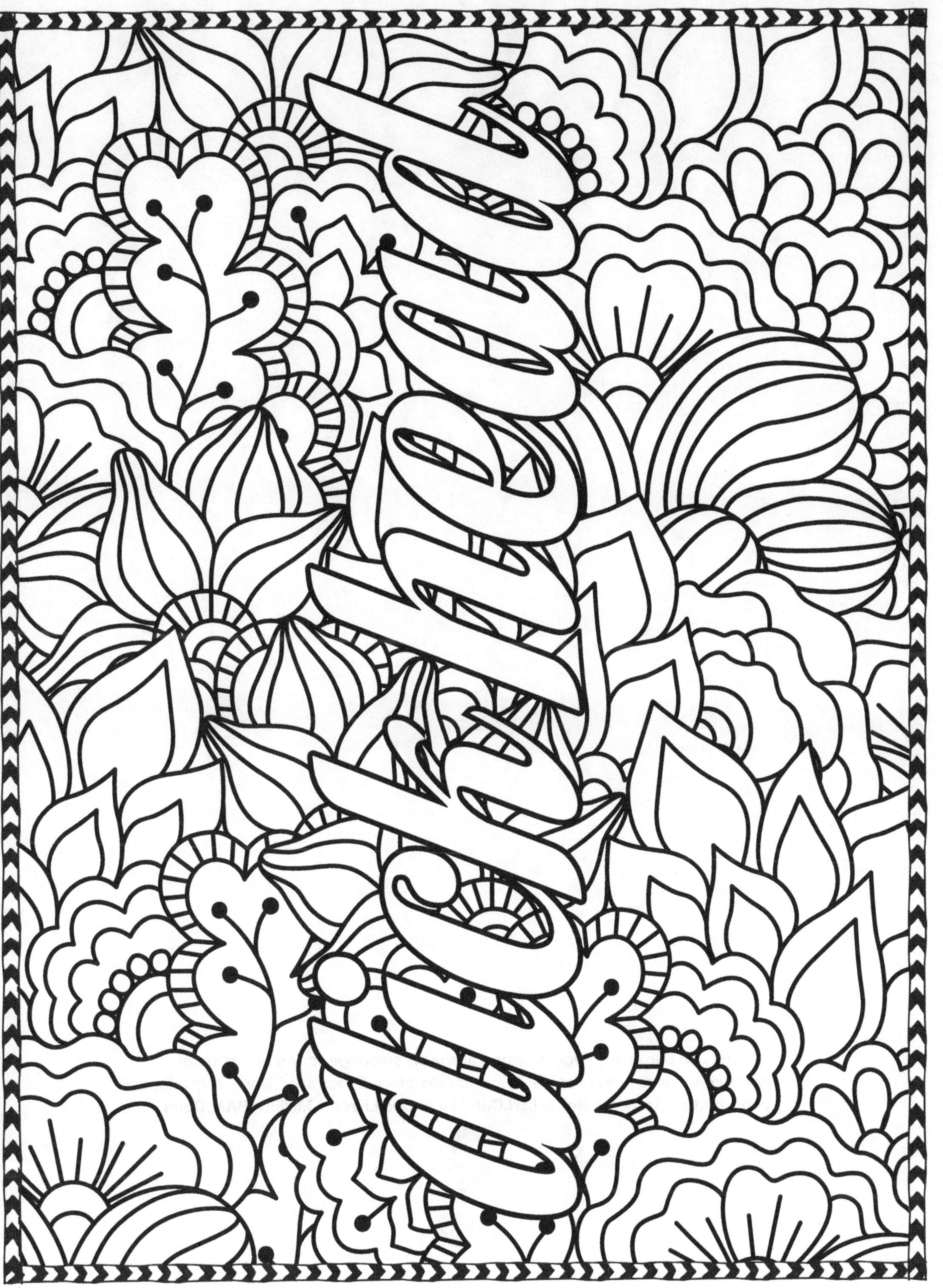

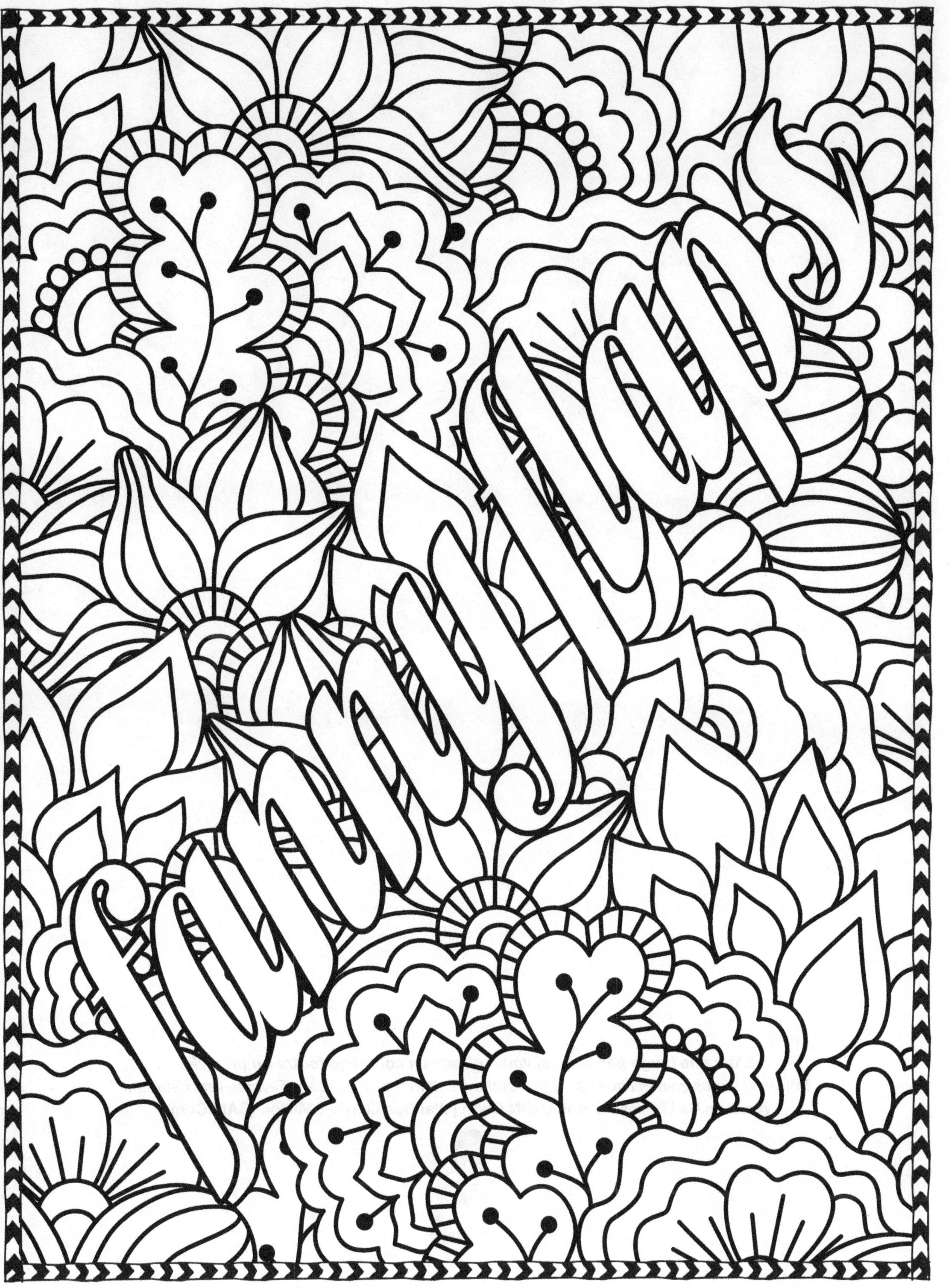

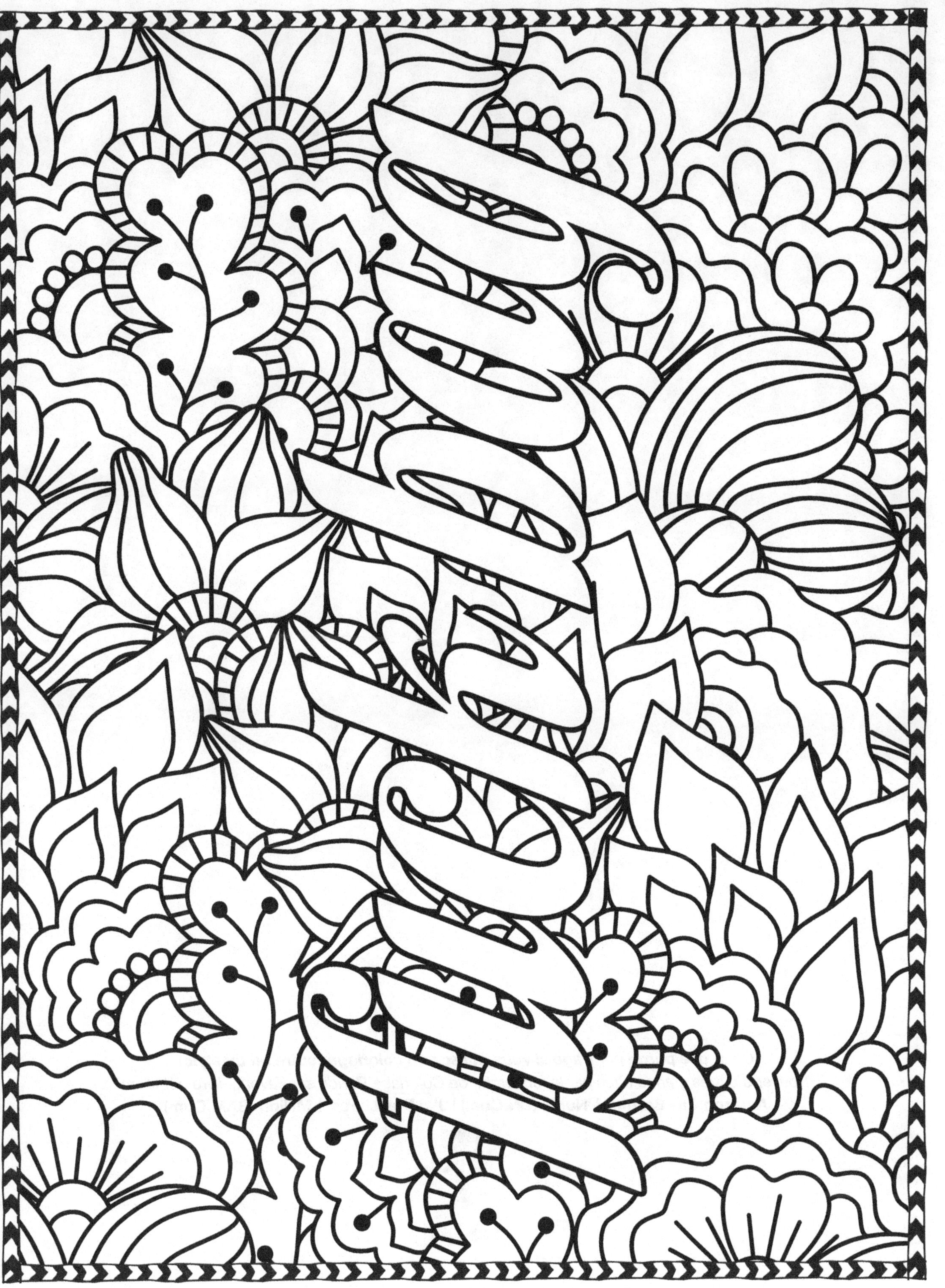

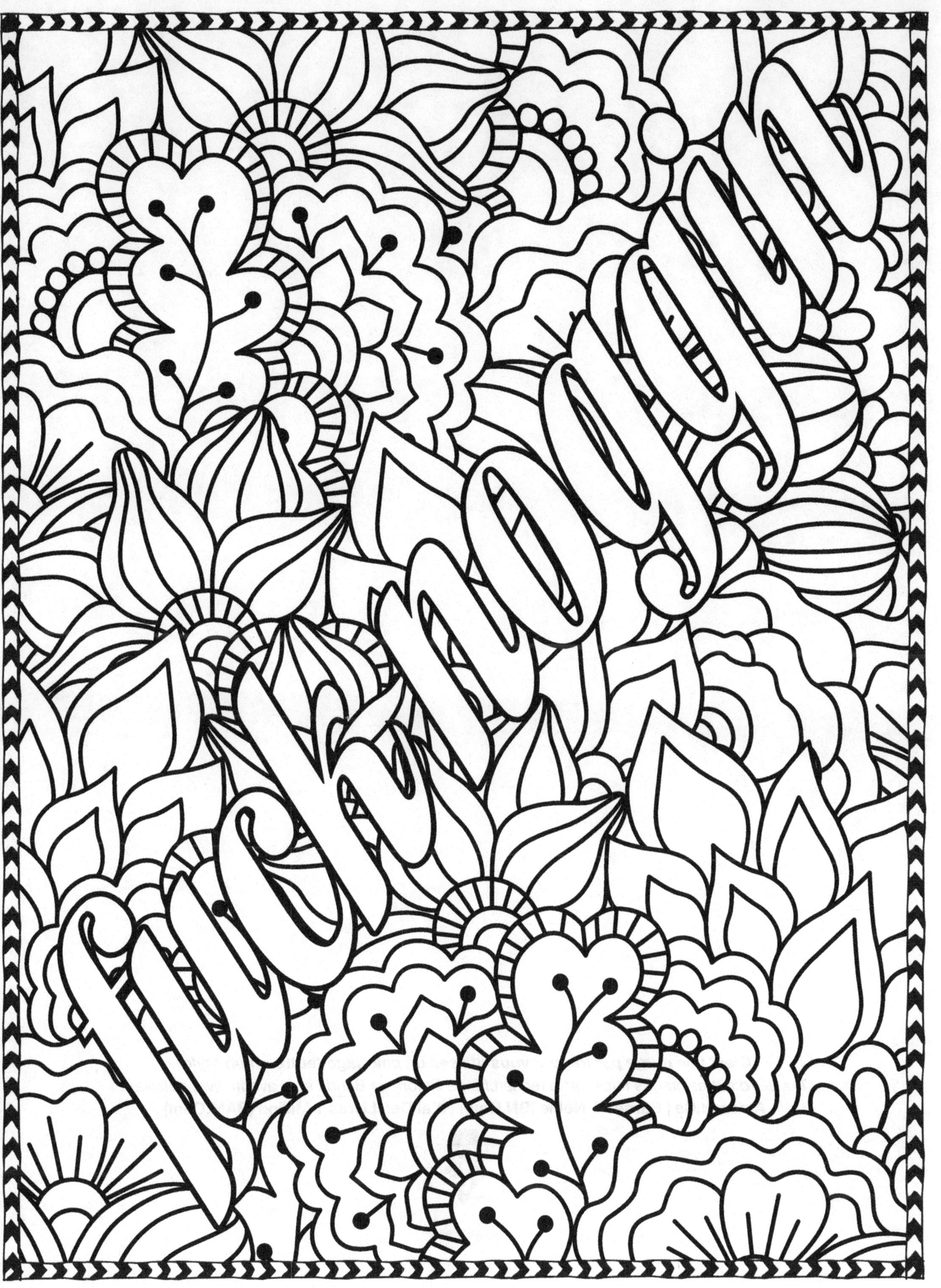

fuck you

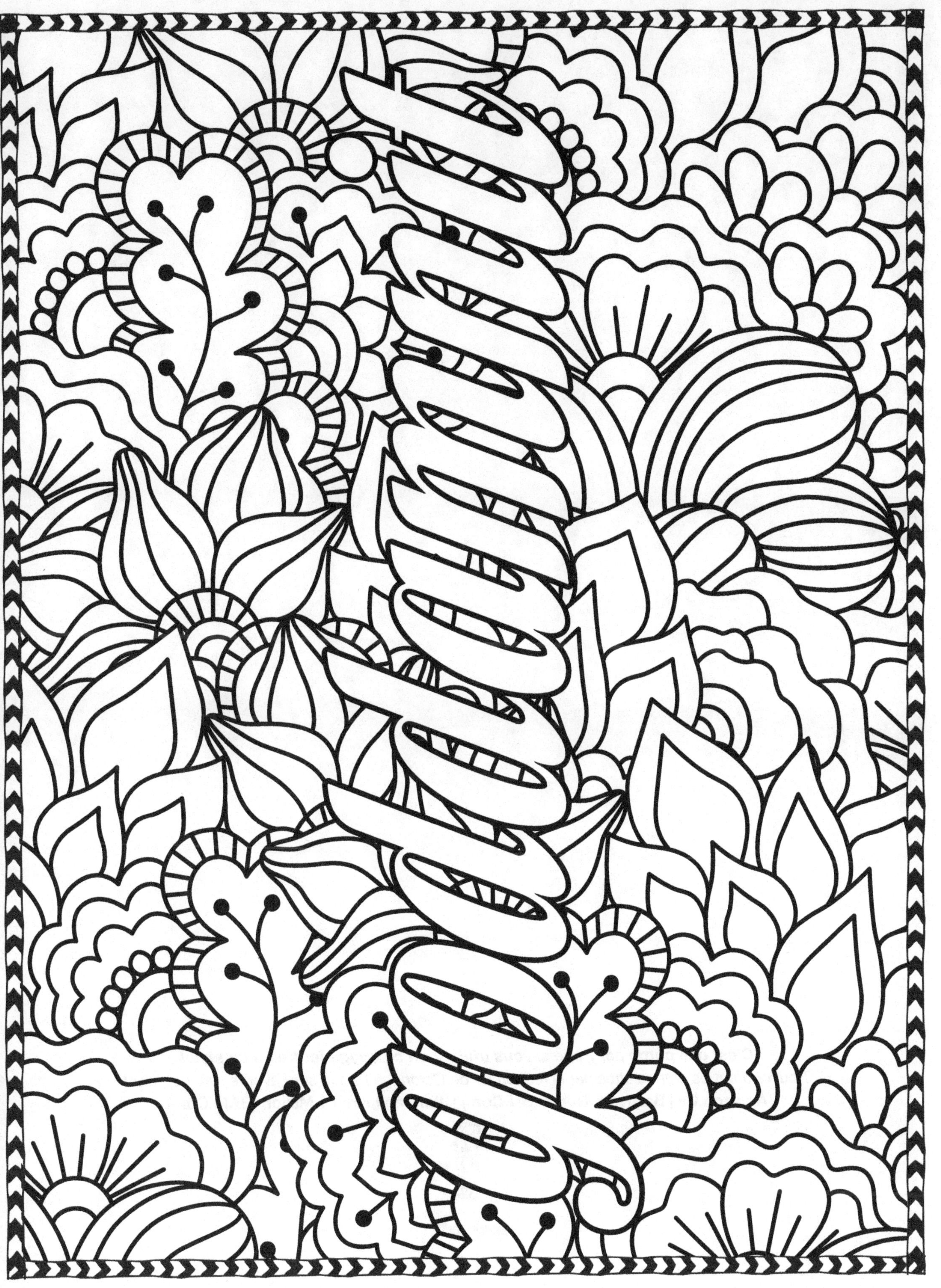

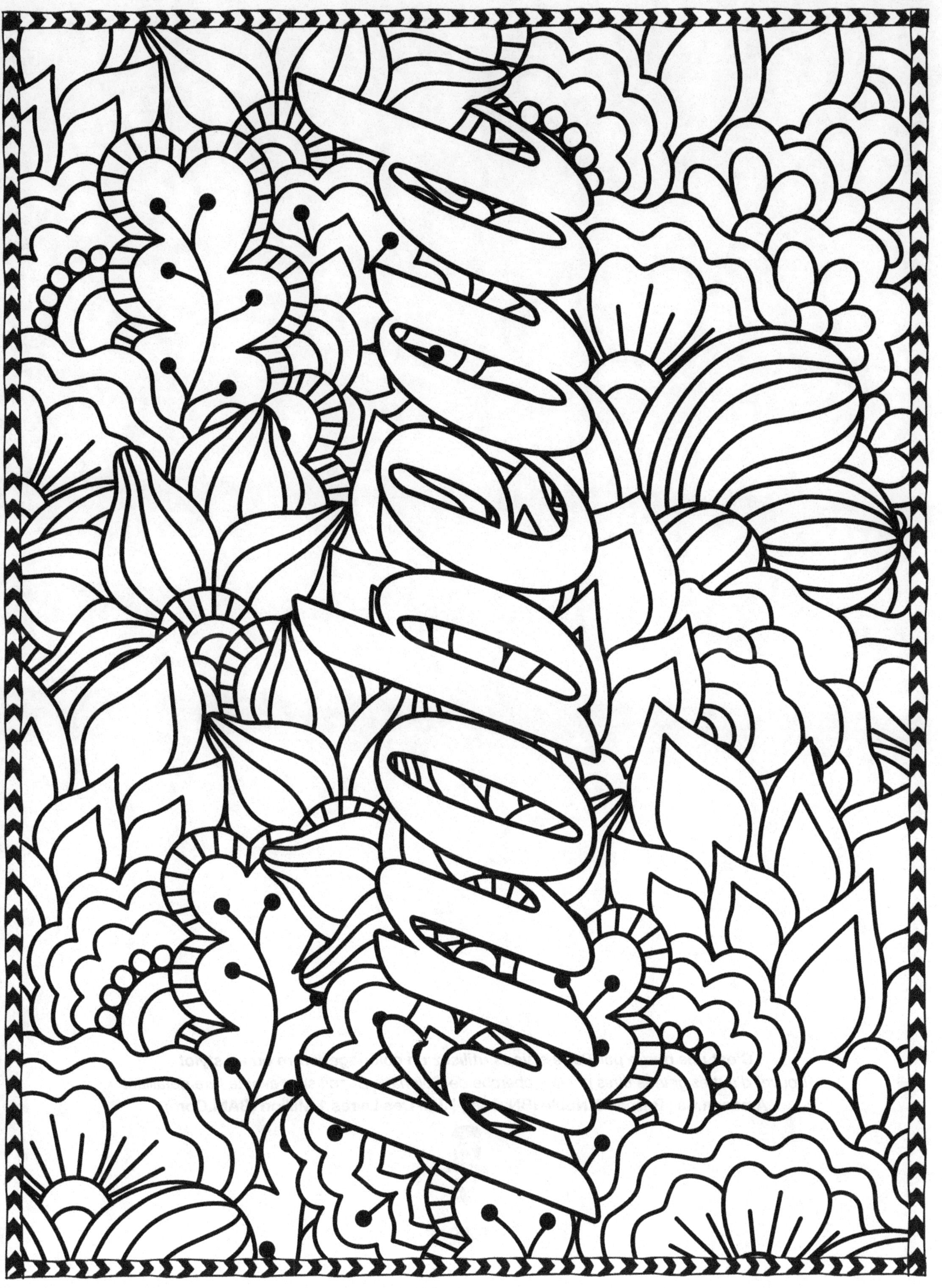

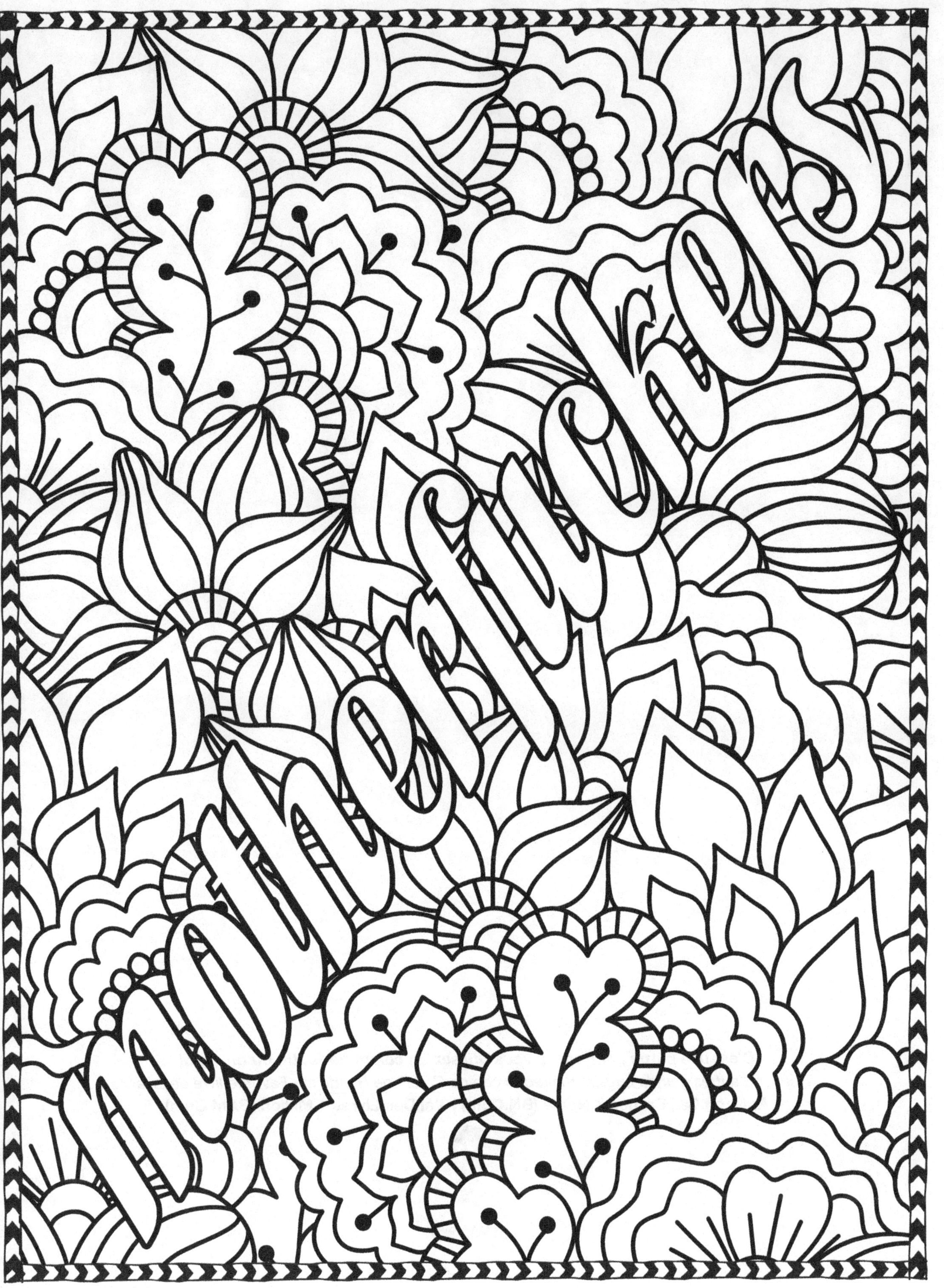

motherfuckers

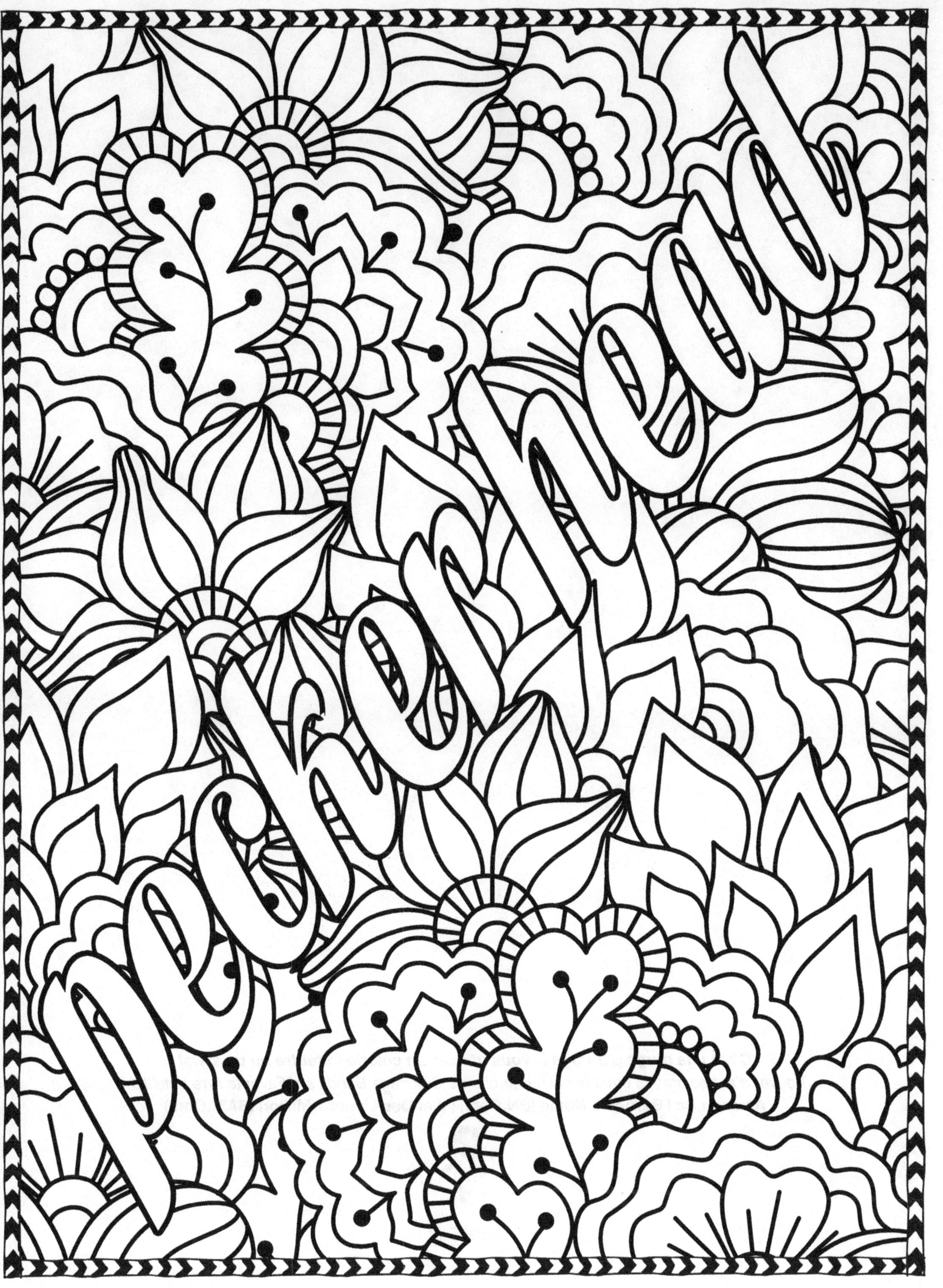
peckerhead

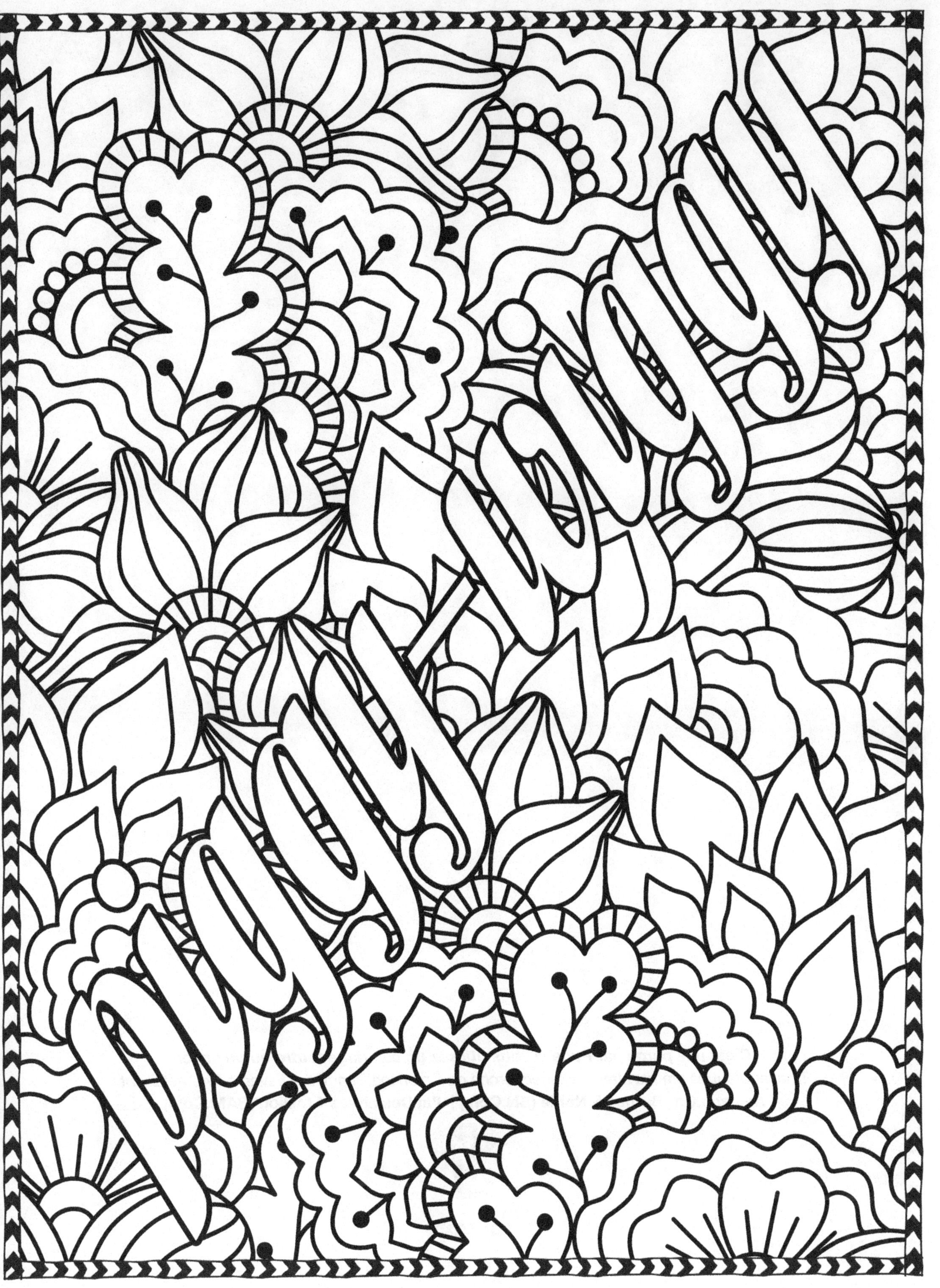

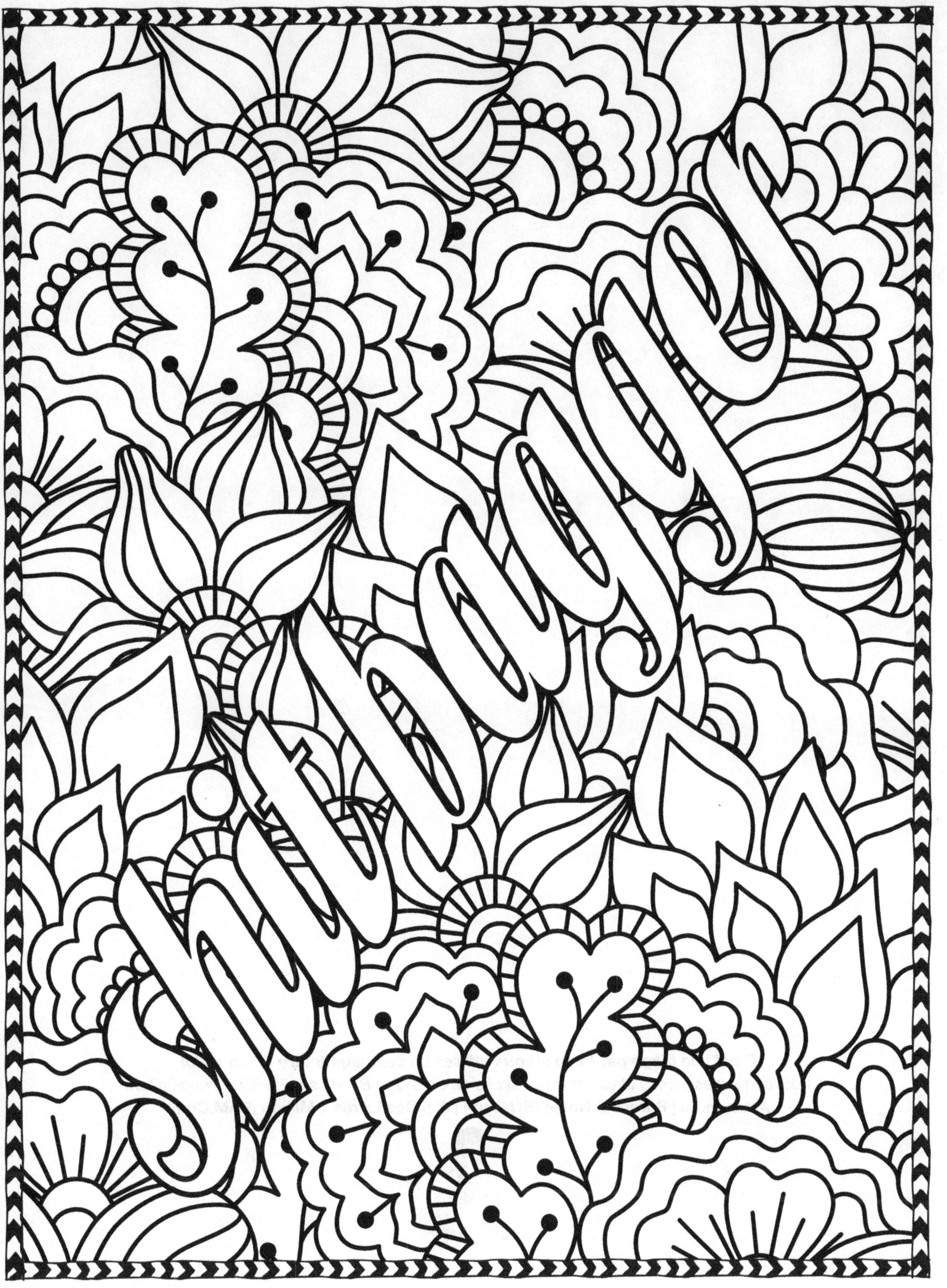
You bugger

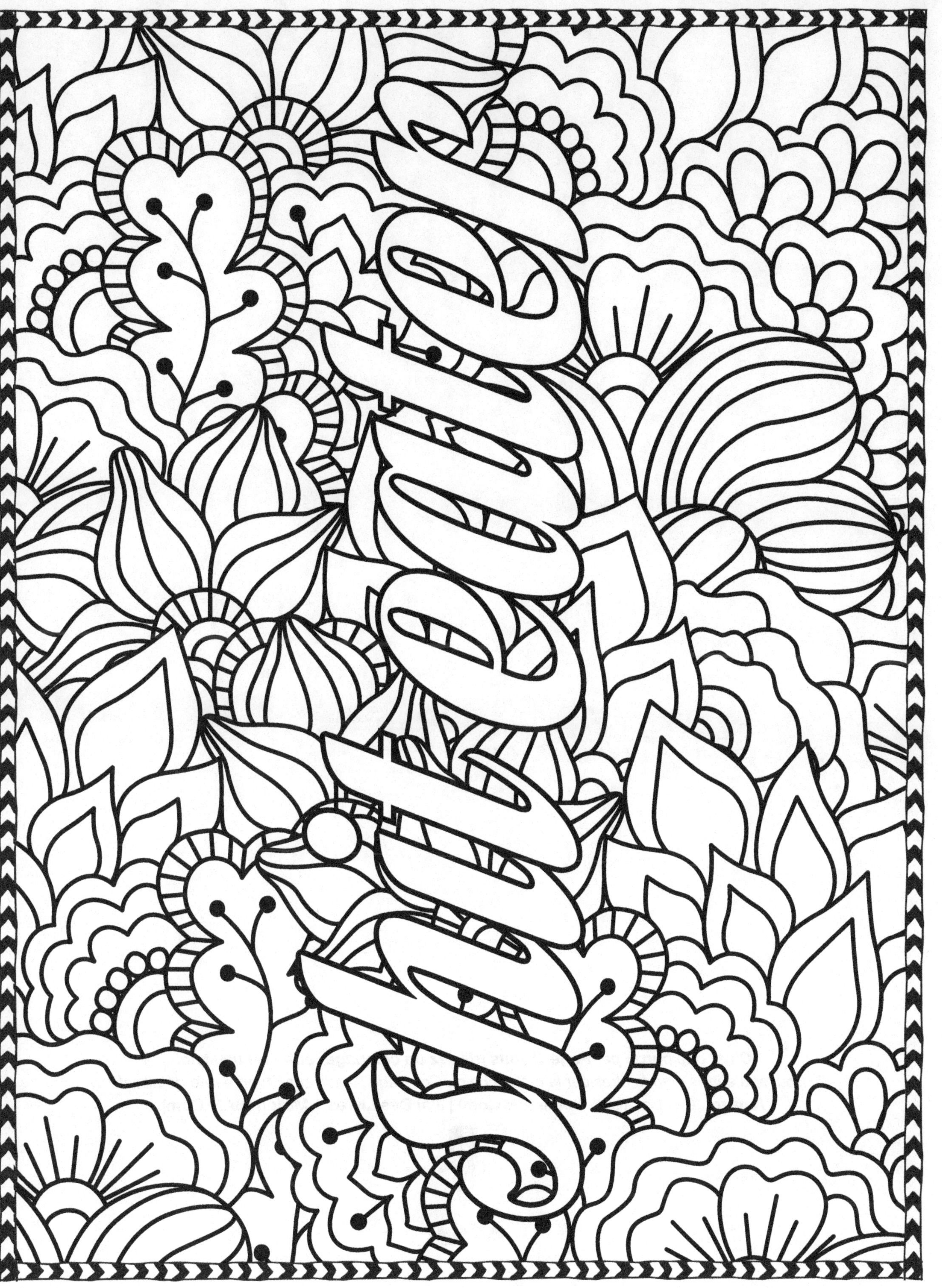

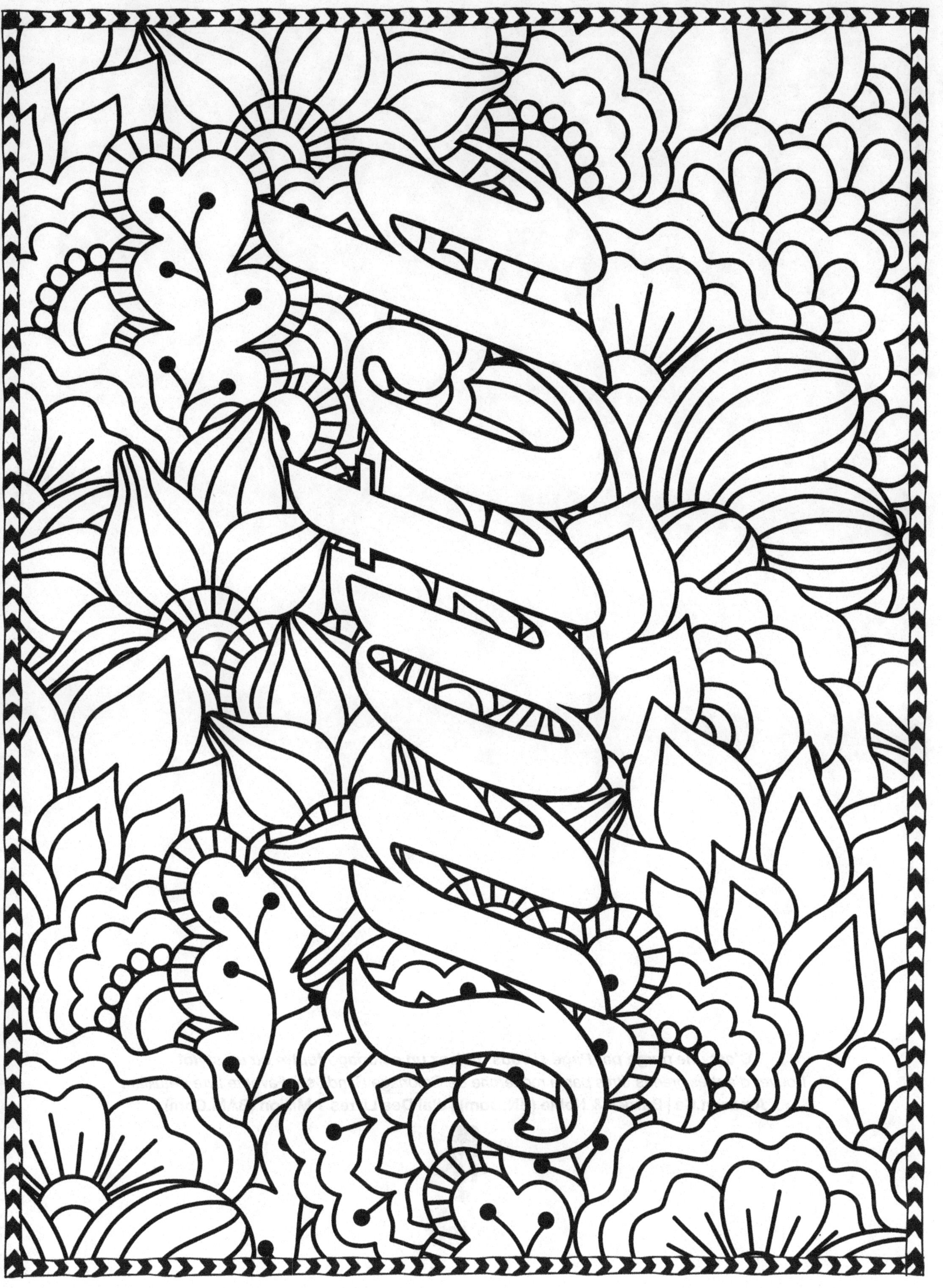

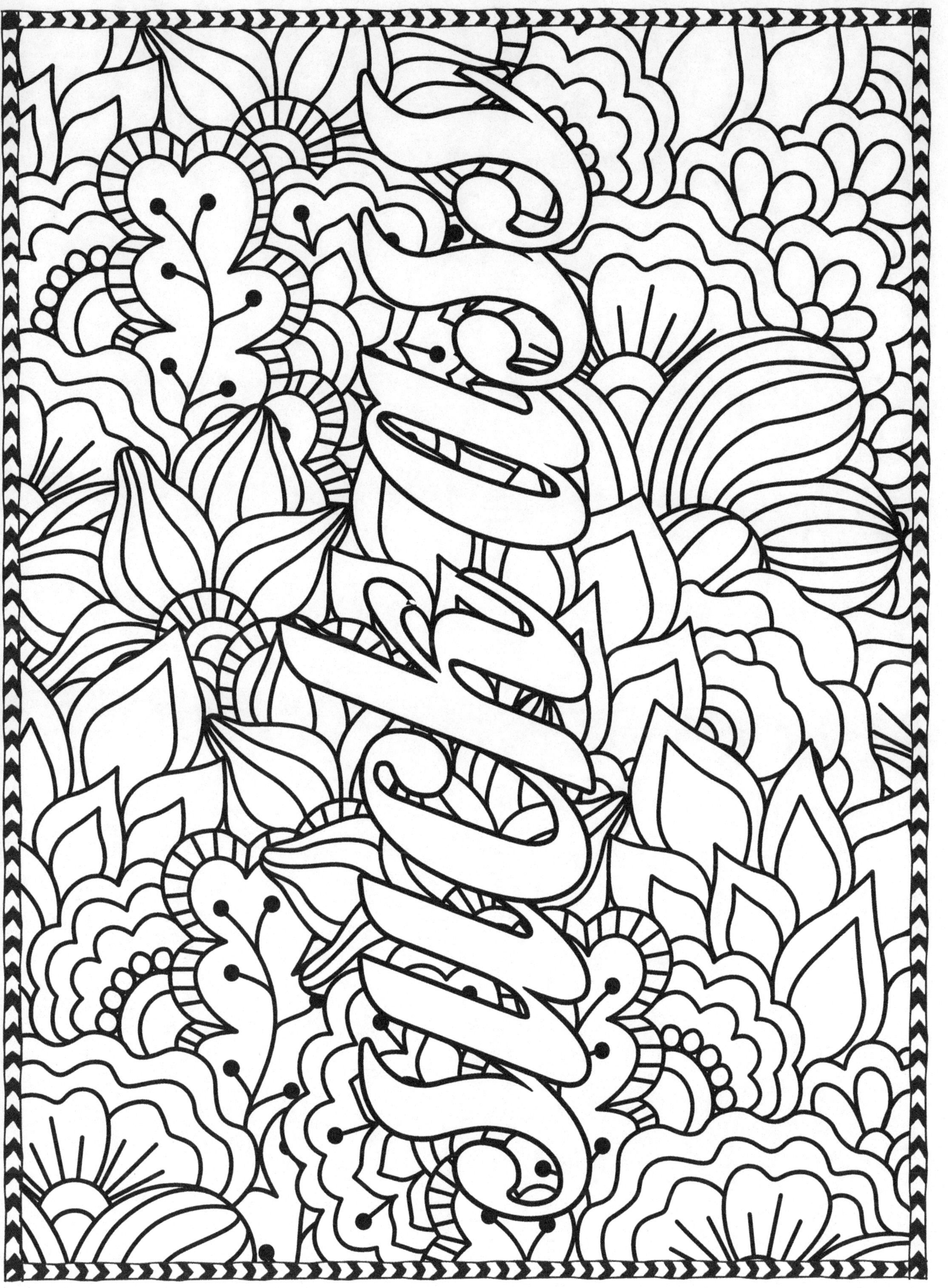

Made in the USA
Monee, IL
07 July 2026

56545437R00059